AF592876

WISH WE WEREN'T HERE

Books by Barry Waters

PISTE AGAIN: A Guide to Survival Skiing
THE TENNIS RACKET
WISH WE WEREN'T HERE: A Survival Guide to Abroad

Barry Waters

Illustrated by Graham Thompson

NEW ENGLISH LIBRARY

The Author and Publishers gratefully acknowledge permission to include an extract from 'Little Gidding' in *The Four Quartets* by T. S. Eliot, by permission of Faber and Faber Ltd.

First published in Great Britain in 1984 by
New English Library, Mill Road, Dunton Green, Sevenoaks, Kent.
Editorial office: 47 Bedford Square, London WC1B 3DP.

Typeset by Rowland Phototypesetting Ltd,
Bury St Edmunds, Suffolk
Printed in Great Britain by St Edmundsbury Press
Bury St Edmunds, Suffolk

Waters, Barry
Wish we weren't here: a survival guide
to abroad
1. Voyages and travels—Anecdotes,
facetiae, satire, etc.
I. Title
910'.207 G465

ISBN 0-450-06083-7

Contents

GITA

Introduction

'I hate abroad' George V
'Abroad is bloody' George VI

WHY EVER do we go? All those foreigners with their strange languages, odd food, funny smells, peculiar ways and high prices. They, of course, think equally highly of us. *C'est entendu*. It's not just we little Englanders who don't like being away from home. We all have our abroads.

Most of us, however, fail to be as frank about foreign parts as Georges V and VI. Every year we return home penniless after the annual ordeal – probably to find that the house has been burgled and that the pot-plants have gasped their last. We've been abused, double-booked, bumped, cheated, humiliated, poisoned, misinformed, misdirected and generally mistreated. But somehow, we never quite admit it.

At first, of course, we can't wait to seek legal redress for all that suffering, to dash off our letters of complaint and get ourselves reimbursed for those astronomical medical bills.

But in the end it never seems to come to much. The sunburn fades, our stomach stops heaving and we resign ourselves to not getting our money back. The photos are gummed into the album and before long we find ourselves inflicting them on our friends, and even telling them how wonderful it all was.

Come Christmas, with the papers and magazines full of holiday ads and supplements, there we are again poring over maps and brochures, reminiscing fondly about our summer adventures and gearing up for another crack at abroad next year. Some of us can't even wait for the summer to set foot again on foreign concrete. Off we go in search of winter sunburn, probably on the slopes of some God-forsaken Swiss mountain-top with long boards strapped to our feet.

Why do we do it? It was understandable enough for the explorers of old. They were making history as they went in search of some Shangri-la that they could name after themselves. But it's all been done now, without oxygen, and we can see it all on television.

It was all very well for the upper classes on their grand tours or *voyages philosophiques*, with their letters of introduction in their pockets, as the natives bore them in sedan chairs over the Alps. They could afford it and they didn't have to carry their own luggage. Serve them right if they got the collywobbles or malaria.

But why us? You and me. The plebs. Nowadays it seems we've all got to go. Travellers have long since ceased to be special people. They're us and they're called tourists, or rather Typical Tourists.

The whole world has now become a tourist destination. People even visit Britain, in large numbers, as anyone who has occasion to shop at Marks and Spencer, Marble Arch, will testify. These days, at any given time, about half of the world is in the process of visiting the other half.

The only people who manage to opt out are the top bods, the tycoons amongst us, who can claim they're too busy. ('Can't remember when I last took a vacation.')

The rest of us, with nothing better to do, just keep on hauling the old suitcase off the top of the wardrobe and packing our suntan oil and funny hats, ready for another go around.

We should know better of course. We've all been around enough to know that there are no more Shangri-las to be found and that abroad is like home, only worse. And yet instead of sensibly following Alexander the Great's example – sitting at home in comfort moaning that there are no more worlds to conquer – we trot off merrily on some well-trodden path where many have gone before.

The word travel itself (*travail*/work) is a giveaway. In fact, travel is harder work than work. So what are we still trying to prove now that the battle for annual paid holidays has been fought and won? Is there no way of halting the tourist tide? It seems not. Even in the midst of recession the annual figures for our seasonal migrations keep right on rising. And if the futurologists are right, tourism will be the world's number one industry by the end of the century.

It's now accepted as quite normal that life as we know it should be suspended during the month of August for the *grandes vacances*. Governments and business virtually shut up shop. Even revolutions get halted in their tracks. (Remember how the French revolt of May 1968 ended by mid-June so that petrol rationing could stop and people could go off on holiday?)

Away we go on our annual outing, like lemmings to the slaughter (that's another thing about travel – you start mixing your metaphors and forgetting your own language), Michelin in hand, holiday hat on head, camera primed, Lomotil at the ready, bound for our two weeks in Macchu Picchu or in Golden Samarkand. Yes, you can even go there now on a package tour.

There's no getting away from all this getting away from it all. It's something we must learn to live with – the price we pay for our leisured life-style in today's global village.

Happily though, it need not be quite as bad as all that. There is now new hope for many long-suffering Typical Tourists. Techniques for coping with abroad have been evolving rapidly in recent years. And as a result a growing number of Typical Tourists are joining that once select crop of voyagers known as Untypical Tourists. These are the wily veterans who have learned to avoid the worst, or, at least, to give as good as they get when they go abroad.

The original Untypical Tourists developed their skills the hard way, by suffering and by bitter experience. But it's now possible to acquire many of their basic survival techniques rather less painfully. And that's where this book aims to be of help.

The best advice it can give, of course, is Don't Go. As the Fifth Earl of Cadogan put it: 'Never go abroad. It's a dreadful place.' Far simpler to stay at home, hire a foreign cook, buy a sunbed. After all, Defoe managed to write *A New Voyage Round the World* from the comfort of his fireside in London, without actually having to make the trip. You can always get someone else to bring you back a bullfight poster or an *Alpenstock*. Come to think of it, you can probably buy them yourself in the High Street, cheaper. Why not see the Pyramids in comfort on a screen in your own home? Now that we have videos of all those places, there's even less need to go.

This book accepts, however, that this sort of advice will not be heeded – if only because the neighbours will think we're mean if we don't go away, or, even worse, that we can't afford it. Not that that's any excuse for not going – you can even take out 'holiday loans' now if you're a bit short of the ready to finance your annual trek.

It recognises that nothing can deter the Typical or Untypical Tourist. He may sit quietly at home saving for eleven months of the year, but at a given moment there will be no stopping him from suddenly upping sticks and setting off in search of Keats's 'beaker of the warm South', as ready as ever Byron was to dive off some *palazzo* balcony into the Grand Canal or do something equally daft.

There's no explaining this phenomenon, which has long perplexed the philosophers. Voltaire said it was just a way of learning to love your own backyard. Stevenson said the journey itself is the goal. We won't argue.

This book certainly can't offer any answers. It accepts the essential paradox of it all that though most of us would rather not go, go we must – if only to be able to say we've been. In other words, abroad is awful – but unavoidable.

It accepts that many of us will not return the same people as when we left, and that in the process of discovering *'la différence'*, we are liable to pick up all sorts of funny foreign habits which may subsequently prove hard to kick. We've all got friends, sound Englishmen and -women in all other respects, who've got hooked on something like smoking Gitanes; or drinking espresso coffee for breakfast; or asking for mineral water in restaurants. It's the sort of thing that can happen to any Tourist – Typical or Untypical.

But the Untypical Tourist does at least manage to limit the damage. One way of doing so is not to go too far afield. That's why this book sticks mainly to the beaten track – Familiar Foreign rather than Aloha Abroad.

At all events most Brits know that the real abroad lurks just the other side of the

Channel, where the Frogs and Wops and Krauts and Dagos live. No need to travel by canoe or camel, or to head for Patagonia, or go in search of the Northwest Passage, or follow the Great Silk Road. Conventional travel on the Continent is quite arduous enough. In any case, the basic principles of survival abroad are much the same wherever you go, be it Bora-Bora or Benidorm, Baluchistan or Baden-Baden.

No-one, of course, really wants to go to any of those places. Brighton is bad enough. But come the summer, you can be sure that they'll all be crawling with visitors, most of them suffering more than they deserve.

The Untypical Tourist techniques outlined in this book won't enable you to escape the agony entirely. But, once mastered, they can help you to suffer that little bit less. You won't come back unscathed, but then you probably wouldn't want to. After all, it's generally accepted, by both Typical and Untypical Tourists alike, that the aim is not just to return to tell the tale but also to return with a few tales to tell.

1
Typical Tourists

'Tourists . . . common and worthless people and sad into the bargain'
Hilaire Belloc, *The Path to Rome*

ONE THING that nearly all tourists have in common, whether Typical or Untypical, is that none of us will ever admit to being one.

We're just over visiting friends, or on business, or having a quick look round, or taking a spot of R and R, or passing through. But we're certainly not *tourists*. No fear. Not *us*. Not likely. God forbid. Can't stand them.

It may be that to the casual observer we give every appearance of being tourists. We may behave like tourists sometimes. We may perhaps dress like tourists – with our Kiss-me-Quick hats, and our sandals and our colourful shirts decorated with palm trees and with 'Hallo' written all over them in ten languages. But *tourists* are not what we are at all. *We've* come to pick up a few antiques, or so that the children learn the language, or to help with the harvest. In short, we have a specific reason for coming. And this, we feel, puts us into a different category entirely.

The funny thing is, though, that whatever their stated reason for coming abroad, most people seem to go about their business there in much the same way. They spend their days doing much the same sort of things and keep running into other people not unlike themselves. They could so easily pass for tourists. Could it be that that's what they've been all along without realising it?

If you're beginning to have your doubts about not being a tourist, try going through the following checklist. If you qualify on at least five counts, then perhaps you'd do best to admit that the funny cap you're wearing does seem to fit.

Tourists

- arrive with a camera, an airline bag, a map, a guidebook, a phrasebook and a stick of duty-free cigarettes, wearing a funny hat, sunglasses and a sock-it-to-them holiday outfit
- soon buy another funny hat and native clothes that they'd never dare wear at home
- believe that in this 'typical' garb they could easily pass for one of the locals
- bring with them twice as much as they need, omitting to pack only the things they really need

- think they're enjoying themselves
- suffer most of the time
- misunderstand
- are misunderstood
- are forever asking the way
- queue constantly while the locals push in in front of them
- lose things
- lose their cool
- get lost
- get told to get lost
- stand on windy street corners trying to read their map
- can never work out how to fold their map up again properly
- forget the name of their hotel
- forget the name of their street
- spend a lot of time on pavements outside restaurants studying the prices on menus
- get on and off the local buses by the wrong door and never have the correct change
- try to get tanned
- get burnt instead
- are miserable when it rains
- find themselves reduced to playing ping-pong
- buy very expensive four-day-old newspapers
- discover that the weather's a lot better at home
- see from the temperature chart that the weather's better just about everywhere else in the world
- learn from the locals that the weather was perfect the previous week or the previous year
- get cold and bored at the *son-et-lumière*
- worry about the water being safe to drink
- spend a lot of time buying and sending postcards
- discover later that there are cheaper or nicer postcards in another shop (which also sells stamps)
- never have a pen handy when there are forms to fill in
- frequently find, when they want to buy something, that they don't have quite enough money or have the wrong currency
- see the sort of sights they'd make a point of not seeing at home
- do silly things like kiss the Blarney stone or put their hands into mysterious apertures in walls
- pay good money to ride on a donkey or be driven two hundred yards by a bad-tempered fellow in a horse and cart
- pay over the odds

- pay over the odds and still get the seat behind the pillar or the table by the kitchen door or the room over the disco
- look down on the natives
- discover that the natives look down on them
- discover it's not quite so easy to drink from a *porrón*, to get some sound out of an *Alpenhorn*, or to pick a lobster out of a tank without getting your hand pinched
- fill their address books with names and addresses of other tourists that they'll never see again
- run out of money
- can't wait to get home
- take home something cumbersome that they don't really want, like a birdcage or a samovar
- buy something at the airport with a very conspicuous brand name like Cardin, or Dior, or Lanvin
- return home overweight (luggage and person)

* * *

Well, OK, if you really must stick labels on people, then yes, perhaps, in our own ways, in our own very different ways, we're all tourists, of sorts. But one thing we certainly are not is Typical Tourists. No, Sir. Not us. Not that.

However, if there's any shadow of doubt in your mind on this score, and you want to put your mind at rest, try answering the following questions:

Are you ever tempted by signs which say:
'A nice cup of English tea'
'First drink free'
'Tourists welcome'
'English spoken'

Are you the sort of person to whom the locals call out 'lookee, lookee'?
Are you pleased or insulted if you get taken for a native?
Do you wear shorts, sandals and sunglasses?
Do you have more than one sticker on your suitcase?
Do you believe that because it's 'duty-free', it must be cheap?
Are you on full-board?
Do waiters immediately address you in English even if they can hardly rub two words together?
When you try an unfamiliar dish, are you more likely to say 'Foreign muck' or 'Wonderful, what is it?'
Do you always know what you ordered?

Do you believe that England is the only place where you can get a good cup of tea or coffee?
Would you ever go on an organised tour?
Would you ever go on anything but an organised tour?
Do you believe there's safety in numbers?
Would you prefer to be in a café surrounded by other tourists or surrounded by a group of locals?
Do you believe it when they tell you they always charge double on Tuesdays?
Do you honk when you pass another GB car?
Do you honk back if a GB car honks you?
Do you turn to the TV page in your newspaper to see what you've been missing on telly at home?
Can you go two weeks without knowing how your local football team got on?
Do you buy those concertina postcards?
Have you ever arrived at your holiday destination, or returned from abroad, wearing any of the following: golf cap, tennis visor, stetson, straw planter, Kiss-me-Quick hat, fur Cossack hat, fishing hat, or Tyrolean hat (complete with badges or feather)?

2
Types of Tourism

'A perpetual holiday is a good working definition of hell'
George Bernard Shaw

HAVING ESTABLISHED that you are perhaps a tourist of sorts, you must decide what sort of tourism to go in for. There's now a tremendous range to choose from. Gone are the days when there were basically only two kinds of tourism – Take-it-Easy Tourism and Have-One-Hell-of-a-Time Tourism. (Neither, of course, lived up to expectations.)

In general, it's the Typical Tourists who are always chopping and changing – skiing down Everest one year, on a *Bierkeller* Beano the next.

The Untypical Tourist, by contrast, is not looking for new experiences. He has learnt that it pays to specialise. So he sticks to what he knows. This enables him to stay clear of the more agonising action and to spend much of his time playing one of his favourite roles – that of the Old Hand who's seen it all and done it all before.

To help you decide on the sort of tourism that might be right for you, let's look at some of the available options:

Costa Tourism

Very popular. Main advantage is that you get much the same as you'd get at home, but you can say you've been away (even if it's only to Vulgaria). You then come back a funny colour to prove it. This is the world of sun, sin, *sangría urbanización*, crazy golf, first drink free, Watneys on draught, Tea Like You Mama Make, *perros calientes*, bins on tost, and chips and Bacardi with everything, all consumed to the pulsating rhythm of this season's foot-tapper – usually some sort of Demis Roussos Bouzouki concoction of indeterminate origin. In fact *costas* themselves could be anywhere. There's always the same crowded beach, colourfully littered with fag packets, orange peel and ice-cream wrappings, the same promenade with its identikit bars and restaurants, where you'll be served by cheery swarthy natives of indeterminate origin. ('Where did you go this year? I don't know. We flew.') Some people rather look down on '*Costa* Cheapo' tourism, but that's only because they don't know a good time when they see one and wouldn't fit in anyway.

Conference Tourism

Much favoured by business executives and academics. The basic requirements are that you should wear a lightweight suit plus a badge with your name on, and wander round with a briefcase full of papers and a responsible expression on your face. You will spend part of your time attending some sort of seminar, and participating in one or two earnest discussions about setting the world to rights. This normally takes place in the banqueting room of a large hotel with the tables arranged in a square and covered by a green baize cloth which is held in place by carafes of water. The rest of the time you will spend sampling the delights of whatever else 'happens' to be in the vicinity – be it golf course or gastronomy. This is one of the few types of tourism where people seem to enjoy getting ripped off – possibly because someone else (the firm) is paying the bill.

Tippling Tourism

A holiday you are guaranteed *not* to remember. Can be indulged in almost anywhere, and at any time. But if you need an excuse try going during the *Bierfest* or the *vendange*. The main requirement is that the local booze should be cheap. A typical day would see you sleep through lunch, begin oiling the system in the afternoon, continue lubrication with pre-prandial apertifs, sample a few more of the local liquids with your meal and then keep trying to improve on them in assorted hostelries around town until you retire, legless, at 4 a.m. – possibly after an early lunch, if the hamburger stall is still open at that time of night.

Camping Tourism

The open air. The great outdoors. The romantic sounds of the wind rustling in the trees, cicadas, transistors, children, the clink of cutlery and crockery, the pitter patter of rain on canvas, arguments about who's to do the washing up. Somehow, though, camping is not what it was. No more ridge-poles, and guy-ropes, and dug-out latrines, and rubbing sticks together to make a fire. Camping used to be a serious business – all about survival. Man against the elements. The gear was a serious colour – field-grey or green. Now it's all day-glo orange and yellow fluorescent. They've even got colour tele, fridges and cookers in them there tents. Some four-star sites have plumbed-in drainage and electricity and, would you believe, ready-erected tents. But it's nice to know that some things are still the same – the mosquitos, the drizzle, the damp, the dogs, and, of course, your fellow campers. And you've still got to be first in line to get the hot water and the loo paper.

Villa Tourism

A bit like camping in that it's life, rather than tourism, that keeps you busy, particularly in the early stages: finding the place; humping your gear up the long narrow path (you can never park your rent-a-car outside); finding the people who have the key (they are usually out); getting it unlocked; working out how the cooker, heating and water-system work; discovering that 'sleeps six' actually means 'sleeps six very tiny people'; tracking down the local representative; checking the inventory; acquiring missing essentials like corkscrew, tin-opener, hangers and mosquito spray. Once installed, you may well find that your 'luxury' villa does not exactly live up to the sweet and seductive name it's bound to have. In fact it will probably keep on springing its little surprises to keep you busy and on your toes right up to that final glorious day when you renegotiate your inventory deposit.

Place-in-the-Country Tourism

Much like villa tourism except that instead of renting, here you *own* your own hovel abroad. Thus there are fewer surprises – the noisy plumbing, the overgrown garden, the leaky roof, the crumbling masonry are all too depressingly familiar. But there is the satisfaction, though, that all these little problems are yours, *your very own*. Like many forms of tourism, the notion of it – your 'old farmhouse in Tuscany' or 'little place in the South of France' – may be more enjoyable than the reality. You may prefer talking about it to going there.

There's now a rather downmarket version of 'little-place-of-one's-own tourism' called 'timeshare' – the theory being that if you only own a place for a fraction of the year, it's only a fraction of the hassle. If you read the small print carefully though (and there's usually a lot of it) you may find it costs you as much to keep up your share for a week as it does not to keep up your old cottage for a year.

R and R Tourism

The ultimate in take-it-easy tourism. Go there, collapse and let the world go by. Arrive, get sloshed and let it all wash over you. Turn on, tune in, drop out. This is the sort of tourism people go for when they feel they've really been through the mill. Needless to say it never quite works out as planned. Rest and recuperation holidays are usually a misnomer and something of an exercise in self-delusion since all holidays are a considerable strain. These are no exception.

Do-the-Sights Tourism

Much favoured by Americans. Sometimes known as 'I-was-there Tourism'. The aim is to find a big city, go to the tourist office, arm yourself with maps and guidebooks and subway plans and tourmobile timetables, book yourself onto a few guided tours and then go around ticking off all the museums and art galleries and churches and monuments just to confirm that they're all still in place. Often associated with 'photo tourism', where you have to bring back pictures to prove it. Can be a bit hard on your blistered feet or your swollen ankles and definitely not for people who don't like pigeons. Once again the notion is often better than the reality. Strolling on the Left Bank or Unter den Linden eating your *cassata* is a nice enough idea. What the guidebooks don't mention is the traffic fumes and the locals who all believe their metropolis is the centre of the universe and resent anyone who comes from anywhere different. The best time to go is probably August when a lot of big cities are affected by the neutron bomb syndrome – all the buildings and sights are intact but there are no locals.

Adventure Tourism

This is where you spend a lot of time planning routes and getting equipped, have a lot of jabs before you go, and set off, wearing a bush jacket or padded anorak, for underdeveloped places in a Land-Rover or minibus, trying to persuade yourselves that there is still such a thing as *real* travel, and hoping that you and your group don't run into too many others trying to persuade themselves of the same thing. You will usually aim to subject yourself to extreme something – like cold (arctic), heat (desert), danger (jungle), height (mountains). Disease, or the prospect of it, often looms large on this type of holiday. Even if you don't manage to catch bilharzia by paddling in the local swamp, there'll be plenty of scope for discussion about the best way of removing leeches, about whether gamma globulin really works, and about the probable exit point of the Guinea worm (the eye?). If this sort of thing puts you off, you can always stick to slightly less adventurous adventures in Europe, on barge, balloon or yacht.

Health Tourism

For the real masochists. It used to be just the aged and infirm who would spend time in a spa going for walks, breathing deeply, taking the waters and having the occasional mudbath. But now you find hypochondriacs and health freaks of all ages. For the ascetics, there are exclusive country mansions, or remote sanatoriums where underweight medics with impressive titles and white coats warn you about saturated fats and sodium, and charge you a great deal for the privilege of being starved, weighed, pummelled and getting very very bored. For the hearties the set up is all much more sporty. Plenty of jogging, swimming, gymnasiums, exercise machines, saunas, jacuzzis, whirlpools, hydro this and balneo that, sunbeds and newfangled racket games. The staff are also rather more jolly but they too charge you a great deal for not giving you much to eat and for talking to you about blood pressure and cholesterol levels.

Activity Tourism

This is very much the trend these days with tourism becoming increasingly more specialised. It's based on the premise that happy is the tourist who has something specific to do on holiday – like play golf, learn a language or buy three years' supply of underwear at Marks and Spencer.

Not that the trend towards activity tourism is all that new. In the Middle Ages there were pilgrimages and wars where people sallied forth with one main aim in view. And there have long been specialised sporting holidays – originally, of course, hunting, shooting and fishing. Now the list is endless – everything from the classics like tennis, golf or birdwatching to more exotic sports like rock-throwing or river-running.

These days, it would seem, there are very few human activities which are not the stuff of which holidays are made. Gastronomes can go on gourmet tours or enrol at *cordon bleu* schools. Old soldiers can tour graveyards, battlefields, prisoner-of-war camps and concentration camps. Western fans can play Cowboys and Indians and live in ranch or teepee on special holiday 'ranges'. Crime buffs can go on who-dun-it weeks. Literati can go on Proustian tours. Snobs can pay a lot of money to stay in a stately home, be entertained by titled persons (or possibly Barbara Cartland) and go to Ascot and Henley and all the right garden parties. Self-improvers can learn to do just about anything – from public speaking to computer-programming. You can go on furniture-restoring holidays, weather watching holidays, stamp-collecting holidays, brass-rubbing holidays, patchwork-quilt-making holidays, corn-dolly-making holidays, or soft-toy-making holidays. You can go on change-your-life holidays by taking up Zen Buddhism, living on a Chinese commune, meditating, or getting an abortion. Or you can go on risk-your-life holidays – for parachuting, skid control or survival training. If you have no desire whatever to either risk or change your life, there are 'professional' holidays – tours for solicitors, accountants, watchmakers, cobblers, undertakers or bankers – thus bearing out Noël Coward's dictum that for many people, work is more fun than fun.

Costa 'Club' Tourism

A specialised form of *costa* tourism. There are now *costa* 'camps' or 'villages' (a sort of cross between Butlins, the Club Med, and Colditz), for boozers, or all-over tanners, or ravers, or xenophobes, or sex maniacs – couples or singles, straight or gay. Brochures for these 'club' holidays are usually written in appropriate nudge-nudge-wink-wink style (with a lot of the sentences ending in dots), and are often aimed at the younger age-groups – say under thirty. This may be because only the younger age-groups tend to have the stamina for this kind of tourism and the vigorous tribalism it entails. Social life tends to revolve around 'beach parties' and sangría-drinking marathons in your encampment, where the aim is to show that your tribe can outdrink, outeat, outfornicate and outchunder any other tribe or club in the vicinity. It's all a bit like *Jeux Sans Frontières*, but with rather cruder games – pissing onto passers-by from balconies, throwing one another and the furniture into swimming pools, etc.

3
Booking Up

FRIENDLY HOTEL
QUIET LOCATION, PEACFUL
SEAVIEW, HANDY FOR THE
BEACH.
SURFKING

'The people you prefer to fly from'
Advertising slogan of a firm of travel agents in Margao, in Goa

WHATEVER KIND of tourism you go in for, at some stage you will probably avail yourself of the 'services' of a travel agent. For most Typical Tourists, it's in his office that the annual ordeal really begins. They've spent the best part of the winter anxiously poring over the guidebooks and brochures, and now it's time to pay their money and seal their fate. Very few have any real notion of what they're letting themselves in for.

The Untypical Tourist, however, does have a pretty shrewd idea. Among other things, he has the advantage of having picked up a smattering of brochurese – that somewhat elusive *patois* that most travel agents and tour operators insist on using when talking holidays.

It's certainly worth spending a little time getting to grips with this particular linguistic code. To give you the general idea, here's a list of some of the more common usages:

inclusive tour	package holiday
villa	small house or flat
Grand Hotel	undusted chandeliers, musty smell, curling carpets
quiet location	miles from anywhere
centrally situated	noisy through-traffic
budget	cheap
standard	substandard
no frills	that's not all it doesn't have
realistically priced	expensive
much sought after	even more expensive
for which a small charge is made	so much for all-inclusive prices
well situated	on main road
good communications	next to railway or bus station
compact	very small
interesting	ugly
animated	noisy
popular	crowded

bustling	even more crowded
unspoilt	don't you believe it
distinctive	eccentric style
charming	window-boxes and shutters
colourful	what isn't?
peaceful	boring
friendly	nothing much to see
traditional	old
retaining all its original character	even older
typical	overdecorated
envigorating air	exposed position
secluded and exclusive	a long way from anywhere and expensive with it
comfortable	run down
easygoing	sloppy
children catered for	hamburgers and chips on the menu
conference facilities	full of men in suits with badges, and expensive tarts at the bar
dramatic position	perched on the edge of a cliff or mountain
newly remodelled wing	but is this where your room will be?
seaview	from how many rooms, and do you need a telescope?
rustic	low beams, dry rot, oxen yokes on walls, landlord with large moustache or sidewhiskers
a firm beach with sand out to sea, popular with the locals	the beach is stony, dirty and crowded
5 mins beach	by foot, bus or Maserati?
within easy reach of	ditto
a few minutes from	ditto
well placed for	ditto
a short stroll from	ditto
handy for	ditto

To get an even more accurate picture, the Untypical Tourist often asks to see the travel trade's own gazetteer, which the agent usually keeps behind the counter. This usually reveals that whereas the brochure may say something like 'There's everything you need in select, secluded Ouzo-la-mer', the gazetteer will say, slightly more realistically, 'offers little in the way of facilities and entertainment and rather isolated'.

The problem is that the travel agent may be unwilling to show you the gazetteer and share its little secrets. After all, he has got a living to make and Ouzo-la-mer has served him rather well in the past. It's the sort of place he usually introduces to the unsuspecting Typical Tourist with the words: 'Well, if you're looking for somewhere a bit quieter, what about Ouzo-la-mer?'

It's the same story with all the best brochures and decent free maps. Tourist offices and travel agents always hide them behind the counter so that you have to ask for them. It's amazing how stingy agents can be with their publications. Some even ask you if you intend to book with them before letting you walk out with an armful. Like most middlemen, they only really like to dispense information they can charge for.

But even if they can be a bit misleading, travel brochures do make fun reading in those long winter evenings. All those beautiful bronzed models posing as ordinary holidaymakers, those spotless uncrowded beaches, endless sunsets and happy hoteliers.

They can also provide quite a challenge to the intellect, a test of our travel judgement. What, for instance, are we to make of that artist's impression? Are those flowers real or just put there for the picture? Will they really be bursting out of your window-box when you are there? Are the people in the picture a high-season crowd or a low-season crowd? Was the photo taken at 6 a.m. or 6 p.m.?

The camera may not lie but the Untypical Tourist knows that clever angles and special lenses do have ways of bending the truth, or at least magnifying the amenities. Your bedroom won't always turn out to be quite so spacious as it looked in the picture. The paddling pool may not in fact be Olympic-sized. And it may just be that the so-called patio or balcony off your room is in reality more of a two-foot ledge.

The Untypical Tourist knows also that what lies outside the photograph is invariably more interesting than what lies inside it. What is around that corner for instance? What's the view like from the other side?

The problem is that very often the picture is all we have to go on. And go on them we do. With what care do we study them as we try to make up our minds. We look at the picture of Rhodes. Then we look at the picture of Crete. And then we notice that the inhabitants in Crete (or rather the models) seem to be that bit more attractive. Or the sky seems to be a shade bluer (a better touch-up job perhaps?). Or that the sea seems to shimmer just a fraction more (different lens filter?). So that's it. Crete it is. That's how the big decisions get made.

At all events, you're probably better going by the pictures than going by the text. The camera may not lie, much, but words have been known to. The problem is that travel-brochure writers are obviously nature's optimists, full of beautiful thoughts, the sort of people who make up rhymes for Christmas cards.

Nothing is ever very much less than wonderful. Beaches are always sun-kissed, the shores palm-fringed, the waters inviting, the people enchanting, the sights unforgettable, the sunsets golden, your holiday that of a lifetime. Wherever you go in Vulgaria, they confidently assert, you will feel welcome.

A favourite technique is to take you on an upbeat romp through a typical day, perhaps on one of the optional excursions, which will never be less than a breathless succession of magic moments:

> Start your day with a champagne breakfast or perhaps a dip in the ocean. Then why not join Pepe in our special air-conditioned panoramic bus on a visit to the eighth wonder of the world (welcome drink included), after which he'll invite you to come with him to the casbah and discover the devilish delights of its bustling bazaars before taking you to the traditional revolving restaurant for your traditional revolving lunch.
>
> Afterwards you may want to take a stroll in the romantic old town and perhaps throw a stone down the centuries-old wishing-well, before returning to your holiday hotel in time to relax at the pool with your free Technicolour magi-cocktail specially mixed by Conchita, before having your candlelit dinner at the romantic rooftop restaurant and then, perhaps, heading for the bright lights of Ouzo, and dancing till dawn.
>
> Or, perhaps, you'd prefer to go on one of our popular 'get disgusting' evenings in the hills outside Ouzo. All the booze you can put away for an all-in (and that's not all you will be) price of 100 Krush. Afterwards, you may even want (unlikely, but possible) to take home with you some of the patron's full-bodied red wine (well-known as an excellent furniture polish), or his white (a first-rate insect-repellent). There's entertainment, too, from the best ninety-year-old fiddler in the village and his caterwauling combo on dustbin-lid, fish-bone and kettle. You will, of course, have a chance to show your appreciation in typical local style by chucking the crockery about. We generally return around midnight, after everyone has had a chance to stop vomiting – if we can find the driver, that is; and if he can find his way round those bends back to Ouzo.

When reading those itineraries, the Untypical Tourist has learnt that it's worth paying close attention to the numbers rather than the words – especially on one of those Ten-towns-in-Ten-days tours. Thus, if you see you're arriving in Wondergrad at 11.30 p.m. on Tuesday and departing at 10.30 a.m. on Wednesday after an hour of 'free time' to 'get to know' the town, you can safely assume that quite a few of the wonders of Wondergrad will go unwitnessed – by you at any rate.

Numbers tend to feature rather prominently in travel brochures. Many of the places you will be invited to visit will have a particular numerical charm. One thinks of:

'The city on seven hills'
'The valley of seventy springs'
'The mountains of a hundred peaks'
'The sea of five hundred fishes'
'The coast of a thousand islands'
'The land of ten thousand lakes'

Another favourite device for describing a place is to borrow the name of somewhere more famous with which it has something vaguely in common. Thus anywhere North of the Alps with canals becomes the Venice of the North, or the Venice of the Fens, or Little Venice. Anywhere perched on a rock with a fortress becomes the Gibraltar of the North, or the Gibraltar of the South, or the Gibraltar of the East, or the Gibraltar of the West. Anywhere with pretentions to resemble the French capital gets dubbed Little Paris, or the Paris of the Orient, or the Paris of the Balkans, or the Paris of the Mountains.

You'll also come across a good many 'gateways' and 'crossroads' in travel brochures. Anywhere you go is liable to be the gateway to somewhere else. If it's not a gateway it's almost certain to be a crossroads – where North meets South, where East meets West, where old meets new, where car meets camel, where Christian meets Moslem, and, unfortunately, where Tourist meets Tourist.

4
Where to Stay

'Life is the search for a decent night's sleep'
Christie Brinkley, American model

AFTER YOU'VE decided where to go and what kind of holiday you want, the most important decision is where to stay.

There is, of course, no ideal hotel, or *pension*, or *rorbu*, or *ryokan*, or *pousada*, or *parador*, or *kro*, or *ferme auberge*, or *caravanserai*, or for that matter, villa or campsite or friend's house or cave, or wherever else you may decide to lay you down to rest.

Nor is there any sure way of knowing in advance quite what you're letting yourself in for. Only when you get there will you know for certain whether your bedroom really is as big as it looked in the brochure and whether, as promised, you really can see the sea – without having to use a telescope or craning your neck round the balcony wall, that is.

Nor is how much you pay any indicator of how comfortable you'll be, or of whether the balcony is likely to fall off. Some Grand Hotels – the sort of place that once had a Baggagemaster to help you get your luggage through customs and where all the guests are eighty-plus – are very ungrand indeed. Nor is country any guide: there's nothing uniquely English about Fawlty Towers, or uniquely French about Thurber's 'Hôtel Pas-de-Calais et Pas-de-Confort'.

At the lower end of the scale we've all heard those stories about quaint old stone inns in the remoter parts of Europe where there's a hearty welcome by a roaring log fire and they do a bed for the night and a five-course breakfast, all for half a crown. Unfortunately, these are delights most of us have yet to experience.

For, in the event, both the Typical and the Untypical Tourist is more likely to find things that are wrong with his hotel than things that are right.

Some familiar problems – like rodents, fleas, cockroaches, bedbugs – are found mainly at the less salubrious establishments – the Railway Hotels of this world. (Three o'clock in the morning is the time to get up and switch on the light if you want to see the animal population all scurrying back to their hidey-holes – especially in the bathroom.)

But most of the problems we'll be examining can be found just about anywhere. Any hotel can put you in a room next to noisy neighbours. Indeed you're probably even more likely to hear them through the paper-thin walls of the newest addition to an expensive international hotel chain than you are through the 400-year-old stonework of some modest *relais de campagne*.

The Untypical Tourist knows that a great deal will depend on that first encounter with the receptionist – once you've found your way past the mountains of tour-group luggage piled up in the foyer. The receptionist can be anything from a multilingual PhD to a matronly housemother, from an unshaven sot slumbering over his reservation book, to someone all done up in buttons and bows or wearing the soup and fish.

Once again, the magnificence or otherwise of the establishment will be no guide as to whether or not they will have a record of your reservation. Very few hoteliers can put their hand on their hearts and swear they don't practise 'walking', i.e. regularly referring overbooked guests to another nearby hotel with which they have a little thing going.

Very often their having or not having a room for you is at the receptionist's discretion, depending on how you respond to such questions as 'How many nights are you staying?' and 'Will you be dining at the hotel?' Receptionists are getting rather good at spotting the savvy Untypical Tourist who tries to get a room by saying he's staying for a week, but intends to check out the next day.

At some older hotels which have a variety of rooms at different prices, they like to size you up first and then offer you a room at the highest price they think you're worth. There's no such thing as a fixed price when it comes to hotel rooms. (Some people, of course, like some Americans, do want the most expensive room in the house – the one where Scottie and Zelda slept.)

The price you'll be charged, incidentally, will never bear any relation to the price posted on the back of your bedroom door. But if you query this the receptionist will always be able to dig out some small print from somewhere to justify the difference or will claim he's applying the latest round of price increases which have only just been approved by the Ministry.

They will sometimes try to fob you off with an expensive room claiming there's no other available, adding that they might have a cheaper one the next night. The receptionist knows only too well that people don't like to move rooms once they've settled in.

This, however, is where the Untypical Tourist will make a point of stating emphatically that, in that case, he definitely *would* want to move to the cheaper room on the following night. This may well cause the desk to have second thoughts since this would mean having to wash two sets of sheets (unless it's the sort of doss-house where you inherit other people's stains rather than sleep on freshly laundered Liddell's Irish linen). As a result the receptionist may revise his proposal and offer you the chance to keep the same room at a lower rate.

On this basis some would argue that a room with a double-bed should therefore cost less than a room with twins since there are fewer sheets to wash. But you won't get far with that one. What the Untypical Tourist will be careful about, though, is to specify whether the rate is per person or per room – not always clear in some countries.

Another determining factor can be whether you intend to have meals at the hotel or not. If you intend to have your coffee and *croissants* at the café down the road at one third of the price of the hotel breakfast, it doesn't always pay to be too candid about it.

This initial bargaining at the desk is more important than it might seem. It'll determine whether you're branded as a Discerning Client or otherwise. If otherwise, and they put you in a grotty room next to the loo or the lifts, or over the discotheque or the kitchens, all is not yet lost. Don't just meekly accept your fate as a Typical Tourist and sign the complaints book when you leave. This is your moment to turn into a true Untypical Tourist. Complain. Loudly. Make a scene. And make sure you do it down in the foyer. Don't let the manager come and settle things quietly in your room. Hotels like to avoid public scenes. (The more experienced Untypical Tourist, incidentally, may save himself all this trouble by adopting the continental habit of asking to inspect the room before deciding to take it.)

If they do agree to book you in and accept you as a *lieber Gast*, there will, of course, be the obligatory form to fill in and perhaps your passport to surrender (often held as a sort of collateral for far longer than they have any right to expect).

They'll then hand you your key (usually with a two-kilo bauble attached), or, if you're somewhere posh, hand your bellboy the key, and you begin your voyage of discovery upstairs.

Don't necessarily expect the upstairs to bear much resemblance to the lobby downstairs. A lot of older hotels have found it pays to modernise their lobbies but they never seem to get round to doing anything about the upper floors.

It's in these sort of places that your journey to your room can be quite an expedition, involving so many lifts, flights of stairs and corridors that you begin to wonder if you'll ever find your way back down again.

Lifts are always a problem anyway, especially those with an inner grill door that someone else always forgets to shut properly so that it's always stopping and starting and going the wrong way for no particular reason, and getting blocked by children and chambermaids (in the morning), and drunks (at night).

On arrival at your room, once the bellhop has switched on a few lights, opened a few doors and asked you 'if that will be all, sir', you'll finally discover whether you're getting seaview, roof view or no view.

But your main concern is likely to be the bed. Are you going to have to do battle (like thousands before you) with one of those lumpy sagging mattresses? Or will your stay be made memorable by a bedframe that creaks and rocks so much that you end up putting the mattress on the floor?

What they put on top of the mattress – blankets or duvets or sleeping sacks – varies from country to country. But your biggest problem is likely to be the pillow, which can be square, or oblong, or the bolster type, or built into the sheet and filled with anything from what feels like soft rocks to little more than air and a few feathers. There may possibly be an alternative kind of pillow in the cupboard, but it probably won't be much improvement.

You'll then set about inspecting the other bits and pieces. The more you pay, the more of them there will be. (Whether a place rates as a one-star *pension* or a five-star palace depends largely on how many amenities it can persuade the hotel inspectors that it offers.) Thus in the top joints there'll be a bowl of fruit, even fresh flowers, a welcome note, a fridge or 'mini-bar' with nuts and booze (seasoned Untypical Tourists replace anything they consume from the local supermarket), colour TV, assorted information sheets and brochures saying what else is on offer, newspaper, writing kit, some art on the wall (or possibly a picture of the local dictator), and plenty of mirrors to make the room look bigger. American-style hotels will, in addition, offer a bible, a bottle-opener, a polythene-wrapped toothmug, a flannel, and a cordon sanitaire across the loo-seat. There may also be a few additional gimmicks like a bed that rocks you to sleep when you put a coin in a slot.

One thing you can be sure of, though, is that no matter how magnificent the establishment, no matter how many towels and bathrobes and bath essences are placed at your disposal, you will only ever get one – or, at most, two – little cakes of soap, about an inch square, in a little paper box, that hardly seems worth the trouble of opening.

But the extras are all pretty irrelevant when it comes to judging a hotel. The acid tests are the bed, the plumbing, the night-time noise level and how much doesn't work.

There is no hotel room anywhere in the world where everything works. The big question is whether it's worth the effort of trying to get it fixed. This can present a considerable challenge – particularly in Eastern Europe. Communist hotels seem to want your stay to be a sort of initiative test. Will you succeed in getting the shower fixed, your washing done, the light repaired, the bedspring replaced, the air-conditioning mended and the phone to work before that glorious day when you check out?

The things most likely not to work are the door handle, the TV, the wake-up alarm, the curtains (either they don't close properly or they're so thin that the light just streams through); you will also probably be without a bath or washbasin plug (to stop you washing your own smalls?) and are almost certain to have a very low wattage bedside lightbulb – if you've got one at all, that is.

Your main problem, however, is likely to be the plumbing: hot water that may only appear at certain times of the day and then only as a miserable trickle or as a scalding torrent that you're never able to adjust; chalky or rust-coloured water; toilets that don't flush; 'telephone' showers that you can't hook up properly, or that have a 'four-position' holder, which won't, however, prevent them from taking off at some point in search of a fifth position, drenching the room in the process.

But even if your bathroom does flood and your pipes do make a perpetual noise, perhaps you should be grateful that you do have these facilities at hand. You're better off than being in the kind of hotel where you have to book a bath three days in advance, negotiate for the key with a reluctant *patronne* and then spend a lot of time sneaking up and down a draughty corridor wrapped only in a towel (you'll never have your bathrobe with you) only to find the bathroom always occupied; when you do manage to get in, of course, it will have been well flooded by your predecessors.

Some hotels have tried to put an end to all this corridor queuing (and put up their prices at the same time) by rigging up a sort of plastic telephone cabin of a shower in the corner of your bedroom. This will have a tin base that feels as if it will collapse every time you stand on it, will probably flood, and is almost certain to drip all night.

Another mod con these places often decide to add is that ultimate in luxury – the portable bidet on a fold-up trestle. Still, these can be as useful as a plumbed-in bidet for keeping the wine cool, washing your hair, soaking your feet or washing your smalls (safer than the laundry which will invariably lose or savage any garment you offer them).

But at least all these extras and 'amenities' in your room are included in the basic price – not always so with whatever else the hotel has to offer. Indeed one of the annoying things about big hotels is that you pay over the odds to stay somewhere with all the facilities and then find that you have to pay again to use those facilities – the disco, or the nightclub, or the sauna, or the car park, or the pool, or the tennis courts or the golf course.

Or, even worse, you find that none of these things is in operation. The pool is empty. The tennis courts are being relaid. The sauna has broken down. The air-conditioning is on the blink. And only two holes of the 18-hole golf course are playable.

The question the Untypical Tourist asks himself, therefore, is whether he really needs these things. Does he really need all those shops in the lobby which charge twice as much as the shops in town? Is it important to him to be able to leave his shoes outside the door for a shine; to have an expensive hairdresser on the premises; to be able to make international calls from his room at five times the post-office rate; to pay over the odds for his theatre tickets at the hotel booking agency? Does he really need a resident tennis pro, a casino, a choice of six bars and three restaurants – bearing in mind that you are no more likely to get a four-minute egg for your breakfast when you order one at the Ritz, than you are at rundown Rita's.

And Rita's, of course, may well have something which the Ritz does not – the personal touch; though one shouldn't forget the valiant attempts by some of the American-style hotel groups to 'personalise' with their photo of the 'employee of the month' in the lobby and by putting up the name of anyone they think is important on the Welcome Board.

That isn't to say that Rita's personal touch is always what's wanted. Those charming little hotels built around a bougainvillaea-clad courtyard with 110-volt current, and two steps to stumble down outside your bedroom door, are also the sort of place where the *patronne* keeps you under constant and terrifying scrutiny.

This good lady sleeps on the premises and knows every creak in the stairs, every crack in the wall. She will also demand constant praise for herself and her establishment, which invariably has notices in the downstairs loos saying 'Please leave as you expect to find'. She does, of course, know everything she needs to know about you. (Mind you, that's true of most hotel staff – they're all great people-watchers, especially the *concierge* department.)

Your homely *patronne* will also probably make clear that her establishment doesn't appreciate being unduly disturbed by its guests; for she clearly anticipates that most of her guests will be tempted to misbehave. Like most hoteliers, though, she may have some cause for this assumption. It is far from unknown for people to try to smuggle extra people in after hours or to walk off with almost anything – towels, bed linen, pictures off walls, other people's shoes, waste-paper baskets, ashtrays, loo paper and even fixtures like towel-rails or the bidet. The more expensive the hotel, though, the more likely they are to tolerate these activites. It's as if you've paid for the privilege of misbehaving. (And, anyway, they buy their ashtrays in bulk.)

The sort of hotel where you feel most at home will probably depend as much on your nationality as your pocket. Many Brits, for instance, still seem to enjoy staying in those pre-war hotels that were built for them in imperial days with names like Metropole, Victoria, Angleterre, Lord Byron, Grande Bretagne and of course the ubiquitous Bristol (named after the much-travelled Earl).

Americans will go for those big post-war hotel chains all built to a predictable pattern, with a name that often includes the words Inn or Golf or Park, and which have brightly painted 'courtesy' buses to take you to the airport. The plus is that you do stand a good chance of getting semi-fresh orange juice for breakfast.

Germans like their hotels well organised with a big *Bauer*-style buffet breakfast and are only outdone in this by the Swiss who have the distinction of being about the only people who seem to be able to run old-fashioned hotels where everything works.

Italian and Greek hotels try to make up with charm for what they lack in modernity and fire escapes, whereas the French tend to rely on having a decent restaurant to make up for their proverbially grotty plumbing.

But at least the Grands, the Continentals, the Ambassadors (hotels tend to have names a bit like cigarette brands), the Golfing Inns, the Miramares, the Bellevues do each have a certain character. That's something you won't find in those motel chains that seem to be springing up all over the place – all plastic finishing, strip-lighting, non-working ventilation units and invariably located on a prime site by the motorway.

Your choice of hotel will also depend on how much time you intend to spend in your room. If you're the type who never unpacks and spends about four hours a night in bed, then it may not matter much where you stay.

But if you're the type who is more likely to get woken up rather than to do the waking up, then perhaps you should select with some care. The wiser Untypical Tourist never expects to sleep too much in hotels anyway. If it's not the plumbing, it'll be the traffic, or your neighbour gargling, or the disco, or the creaky stairs, or the drunks trying to get into your room at 3 a.m., or the chambermaid waking you at 6 a.m. And if it's not the noise, it'll be the lingering fumes from the kitchen, or the cockroaches crawling around.

And don't put too much faith in those 'Do not Disturb' signs you optimistically hang outside your door. They certainly won't cut much ice with the chambermaid. They *may* prevent her from actually bashing on your door, but she has plenty of other methods at her disposal for turning you out – singing and chatting outside, ramming her trolley against the corridor walls, turning up the radio in the room next door, and banging any other doors in the vicinity.

The only time you won't be woken up is when you've given specific instructions to be called (especially likely if you gave your instructions to the receptionist before the night-man came on duty). Alternatively, if you've annoyed the desk, they'll get their own back by waking you up two hours early (a favourite deliberate mistake).

At times you may even feel you would have spent as good, or as bad, a night (and a lot cheaper) at a discotheque, or sleeping on the beach, or at the railway station, or on a campsite. But who would you then be able to blame? As we've seen, most tourists like to have someone to take to task for their misfortunes, and hoteliers, like travel agents, do, at least, provide us with that satisfaction.

5
Travelling Companions

'L'enfer c'est les Autres'
Jean-Paul Sartre, *Huis Clos*

IN THE end, as we all know, it's not where you go or where you stay that matters most. It's whom you meet. It's your fellow travellers who will make or mar your holiday. The unfortunate thing is that travelling seems to bring out the worst in people, or, at least, makes them behave more strangely than they otherwise would. Brits, for instance, actually talk to one another in railway compartments when they're abroad. And no matter where you go, you're almost bound to run into just that person from home that you'd most like to avoid. Untypical Tourists, therefore, put a lot of work into learning to recognise at an early stage the sort of people who might be better avoided. The following sketches offer a few examples. (Even though, for convenience, the masculine pronoun is used, very few of these roles are the monopoly of any one sex.)

The Paranoid

Gets his kicks abroad by imagining the locals are after him. Prefers, therefore, to take his holidays in totalitarian police states of right or left. Tends to wander off alone, especially at night, and then come back with tales of how he is constantly being followed by men wearing trilby hats and trenchcoats. Always seems to have a microphone hidden in the chandelier in *his* bedroom, or some shadowy character lurking at the end of *his* corridor. Much enjoys taking all the proper counter-spy precautions – like wearing a money belt, clipping a portable scrambler to his phone, and wedging matchsticks in his bedroom door whenever he goes out. Preferred reading: John le Carré.

The Sex Object

A sort of female version of the paranoid, except that in her case, the locals are not following her to snap up state secrets. They are after her *body*. Tales of her day's exploits will consist largely of accounts of all the unwanted and unencouraged (that's *her* story) attentions she has been getting – a non-stop succession, it seems, of propositions, pinches, pats, wolf whistles, 'pssts', 'come heres' and '*ciao bellas*'. But even though she spends most of her time telling her compatriots how awful the natives are, she's probably the one who'll disappear for three days with your waiter.

The Money Merchant

Always has a pocket calculator with him and a bewildering variety of currencies, cheque books and credit cards so he can get the best possible deal on every occasion. Spends most of his time making calculations on the back of an envelope and telling his travelling companions what the rate is doing today, and what it may do tomorrow, and which bank or exchange office gives the most favourable commission. You'll earn his undying contempt if you change your money in the hotel. Not that all of these speculations and calculations make him a rich man – he usually manages to save himself about a pound per holiday. But it does give him something to do and it makes him feel he's one up on the natives.

The Credit Card Collector

Often the same person. Has a wallet full of plastic cards, all neatly lined up, or sometimes displayed in little plastic windows, which he may be able to open out, concertina-style, to make an even more impressive display. Loses no opportunity to flourish his wallet and show off its contents. Anyone who happens to glance in his direction will then be treated to a lengthy disquisition on the particular benefits of each card and what he uses them all for. The best thing to do is to pair him off with another collector – they can have hours of fun exchanging views about credit limits and comparing cards.

The Bargain Hunter

A close cousin, often female, who also specialises in offering financial advice. Whenever you buy anything, she will ask where you got it, and how much it cost, and then proceed to tell you, with some contempt, how there are better ones, and cheaper, somewhere else. Whenever *she* buys anything, of course, it's at rock-bottom prices after reducing the local merchants to tears with her tough bargaining. She will also want to know how much you paid for *your* flight, *your* holiday and *your* room. She, of course, paid less on her 'special offer'.

The Enthusiast

Thinks abroad is wonderful. Isn't it marvellous the way the people sit around in cafés eating and drinking. Such style. You won't find people eating and drinking like that at home. They still know how to live, these people. We've forgotten. And what an expressive language. They seem to be able to say so much more than we can. Love to be able to speak it. Just look at them talking to one another. Do you know they have seven different words for yes. What a culture – so rich. They've seen it all and done it all, these people. No wonder they're happy to sit back and take life easy these days. They were making microchips thousands of years ago, while we were still swinging from the trees.

The Imperialist

One of the old school. Believes we've still got an Empire, or should have, and that foreigners look up to him because he's an Englishman and obviously knows better. This place is a shambles or is turning into one and the locals haven't got much of a clue about anything. But he's usually prepared to take the trouble to point out to them where they're going wrong and explain in an avuncular kind of way that 'In England we do it like this'. Also always ready to help the locals with their English and explain to them that 'In England we have a saying which goes . . .'

The Missionary

Often American. Often female. Has come abroad to inflict her progressive concerns on the locals, who, it would seem, are blissfully unaware of things they ought to be taking to the streets about. Their ignorance never ceases to amaze – and delight – her.

'You mean, you aren't worried about high-rises?'
'Is there no women's movement at all here?'
'Is there no form of rent control?'
'Haven't you formed a community association?'

It's beyond her how people manage to survive without such things to worry about. Don't the local women realise how down-trodden they are? You mean, they've never even heard of Betty Friedan?

The War Veteran

Seems to have done most of his travelling during the war – the basic purpose of his holiday being to revisit places he first went to in uniform. Spends his time telling you how things looked when he and 21st Corps rolled up in '45. Not a pretty sight, he can tell you. They really went through it, those lads. But despite his accounts of the awfulness of it all, you can't help getting the impression that he enjoyed the war far more than he's enjoying his holiday.

The Organiser

A similar sort of type, always ready to assume group leadership. Particularly enjoys anything that could remotely be described as a crisis when he can go around telling everyone to keep calm and not to panic (no-one is). Always ready to speak for the British, or for 'our' group, to 'find out what the others think', 'to go on ahead'. Can sometimes be useful, though, for getting together a group to share a taxi, booking tables at restaurants, negotiating with the locals, etc.

The Joker

One in every pack, and noisy with it. He's the one who at airport security always makes cracks about hijacks or the bomb in his suitcase and then tries out his imitation of the noise of the metal detector. Is forever rechristening people with some devastatingly witty nickname: 'Look at old Speedy Gonzales over there' or 'I see Popeye's at it again'. The local currency – funny money or Mickey Mouse money – is always good for a laugh, as are the locals themselves. Most of his 'jokes' are at their expense – usually some mildly insulting remark about them made in quick colloquial English so they can't understand. After any dealings with anyone in uniform who looks vaguely efficient, he'll wait till the official turns round, then click his heels together Nazi-style and wink at you.

The Border Crosser

Gets his travel kicks from crossing borders, clearly imagining he's the original 'man between'. As soon as you approach a frontier zone or a customs shed he'll start chattering away, the adrenalin flowing, about nail-biting border-crossings he has known. Usually tries to smuggle a little something through just to give himself some extra excitement. He may seek to engage you as an accomplice in this, whispering to you in a conspiratorial voice, as if he's about to hand over the microfilm: 'Look, if you're a bit light on the booze, you wouldn't mind, would you, just taking this half bottle through for me.'

PHRASE
BOOK
ENGLISH
GERMAN

The Linguist

Has been taking evening classes over the winter, so he'll probably show off by being the only member of your party ostentatiously carrying a copy of the local newspaper. Will almost certainly appoint himself as spokesman for your group, taking over when there's no proper guide about, and upsetting waiters who speak perfect English by insisting on addressing them in what he imagines the local lingo to be. When he's not busy interpreting, he'll be giving the rest of the group language lessons. Often gets his comeuppance when translating Latin or Greek inscriptions, and someone happens to have a guidebook handy with the *correct* English version.

The Lush

For him, travelling is synonymous with drinking. What better way of passing the time when there's nothing much else to do. Always has a hip-flask, or at the very least, a few miniatures about his person, in case there's no bar handy. But he won't always admit he's just come abroad for the cheap plonk. He may claim to be on a serious 'tasting' expedition to sample some of the region's celebrated *crus*, or to see what this year's vintage is like. Or he's a CAMRA member, well-versed in the difference between top-fermented beer and bottom-fermented beer, and just over to sample some of the local *Trappiste* brews.

The Bar-Pillar

Another type of tippler, always to be found shoring up the bar. It's his station in life. Whether in hotel, nightclub, boat or wherever, the bar is where he makes for, placing cigarettes and lighter on the counter to mark his spot, sliding onto 'his' stool, and propping himself up on his elbows. Barmen are his best friends – they're about the only people who talk to him. Although he usually starts a session with a bright and breezy 'Set 'em up, Joe', the mood invariably turns melancholy, as he and the barman reminisce about bars they have known and commiserate with one another about the luckless hand that life has dealt them.

The Jogger

Invariably wearing sneakers and a sweatshirt, with a number or something written on the back. Often appears at unexpected times – just as you're having dinner or sitting down to breakfast – all done up in his jogging gear, brow glistening with sweat. Doesn't talk about much else but jogging and how it's completely revolutionised his life. His main concern about abroad is that it's completely interrupted his training schedule. He's had to reduce his mileage to a hundred miles a week and this foreign food isn't the best preparation for the carbohydrate loading he's going to have to do as he gets ready for the Croydon marathon.

The Business Traveller

Will be wearing a suit, carrying a briefcase and the *Financial Times* and trying very hard to look like one of the people who run the world. If you have the look of a tourist about you, he'll lose no time in making it clear that he's not engaged in some frivolous pursuit like travelling abroad for fun. Out of the briefcase will come all his important-looking documents, his pocket calculator and his silver-plated biro. If you do strike up a conversation, he'll invariably start talking about 'The firm' (his) and how he reckons he travelled half a million miles last year – at the firm's expense, of course (he's not above trying to make you feel envious).

The Life-Story Teller

Often women. Travel for them is an opportunity to inflict on people who haven't heard it before the story of the trials, tribulations, traumas and tragedies of their life, and how much they've suffered. Again, best to pair them off with someone similar so they can swap stories about the dramatic moments of their marriages and divorces ('And then I saw what a bastard he really was'), about their current companions, and the philosophy of life they've developed since the divorce.

The Overlander

Another story-teller. When he talks about travel he means Big Travel with a capital T. His life seems to have been a succession of expeditions, running rapids, crossing deserts, climbing mountains, shooting bears, frequently snatching his life from the very jaws of death. It seems a bit odd, therefore, that he should be riding along with you to the Costa Sur La Mer, but it seems he's decided to take it easy this time.

The Counter Culturalist

A travelling salesman for the Alternative Society, and appropriately dressed for the job – denim, cheesecloth, headband, beads. Tends to wax philosophic about the whole notion of abroad – 'The road' means freedom, etc. Has two main topics of conversation. Either 'hassles' experienced with foreign officials and sundry other 'Fascist bastards'; or 'memorable moments' abroad – fantastic freak-outs, great one-off lorry lifts from Croydon to Kathmandu, sunrises, sunsets, making love under moonlit waterfalls, etc.

The Family

The couple with a brood of brats who are allowed to run riot and clamber all over everyone else. The parents seem to feel this provides the rest of the company with immense entertainment and pleasure, even for people who have children of their own. Fortunately there will usually be some lone woman around eager to play Auntie and act as a decoy by offering them sweeties, picking them up, and asking questions about their age, sex, etc. Not that this will subdue them for long, any more than the shrill injunctions of their parents. ('Will you please sit still', 'If you do that once more', 'When I say No I mean No'.) The only sure way of getting some peace is to slip several paediatric sedatives into their Coca-Cola.

The Vehicle-Vetter

These people are nuts about trains, boats, planes or anything on wheels that moves. They carry little spotters guides in their knapsacks and their greatest joy is to catch sight of some rare aeroplane, automobile or locomotive, the like of which is not made any more. These experiences will all be diligently recorded in a notebook. It's often difficult to know exactly what they're on about since most of the things they talk about will be referred to by numbers and initials. Airports, for instance, are always JFK, CDG, TXL, FCO.

The Jockeyer for Position

This person either has to be the first on board, or first off, or last on, or last off. He often likes to drag someone else (like you) along with him, as he puts his theories to the test, explaining, for instance, how last will in fact mean first when it comes to unloading or getting fed. If they are working on the 'last shall be first' theory, they tend to be last very ostentatiously, sitting back with book or newspaper while everyone else crowds into the aircraft gangway, and remarking: 'Why all the rush? Can't understand some people. We'll all get there in the end.'

The Name-Swapper

Usually starts conversations with 'Where you from?' and then gets on to where else you've been. His purpose is to identify places where he's also been and where he knows people, on the assumption that you probably know them too: 'You don't say.

Small world. We have friends in Vancouver. You don't know the Smiths, do you – John and Anne? Lovely people. Met them in Tahiti last year.' If you don't know these particular Smiths you will be asked to look them up and give them a message. For obvious reasons, it's advisable, if you can avoid it, not to give the name-swapper your address.

The Investigator

This tourist is not just on the trip for the fun of it. He's a serious traveller. He came to find out about the country and the people. He's therefore constantly collaring the tour guide and asking him questions he can't answer about the growth rate, unemployment, inflation, the situation in the textile industry, the circulation of the local newspaper, etc. He'll opt out of the more frivolous excursions in favour of something rather more instructive; instead of going on the booze-sampling tour he'll go off to visit the local bottle-washing plant.

The Passport-Comparer

His proudest possession is his passport. If you asked him to, he could recite by heart exactly what Her Britannic Majesty's Principal Secretary of State for Foreign and Commonwealth Affairs requests on behalf of its bearer. He's even prouder of the stamps inside it (if a border official doesn't give him a stamp, he'll make sure he asks for one). He will usually begin a passport discussion with you by comparing photographs and will then proceed to invite you to admire his collection of stamps, explaining exactly how and when each was acquired. He will, of course, take a polite interest in any stamps you may have to show him.

The Sufferer

A living example of the dictum that to travel is to suffer (he'd never believe that in the old days people used to go abroad for the good of their health). Is invariably hung over, or suffering from heatstroke, or the local variety of 'Turista' (Delhi Belly, Turkish Trots, Gippy Tummy, Montezuma's Revenge, Kathmandu Quickstep, etc.). But he usually asks for it. On arrival, he starts bouncing around like a squash ball in heat, and living off the local equivalent of steak tartare, or the special mercury-rich shellfish, and washing it all down with something like grappa or Tequila.

The Hypochondriac

Has a medicine chest with him that the flying doctor would envy. 'Abroad is dangerous for your health' might be written on the side. Also fully equipped with forms E 111, and other assorted *feuilles de soins, Krankenscheins* and medical insurance policies. Makes sure all water is boiled in front of him, drinks with his lower lip inside glasses or bottles, brushes his teeth in mineral water, and always asks if the milk is pasteurised. His greatest pleasure is warning you about the local bugs and diseases you are exposed to. He also enjoys having abstruse discussions with the local pharmacists, finding out the local name for Mistura Kaolin or Magnesium Trisilicate, or some other drug he needs to add to his collection. If you need an aspirin he's the man to go to.

6
Foreigners

'The English, the English, the English are best.
So up with the English and down with the rest'
Flanders and Swann, 'A Song of Patriotic Prejudice'

OF COURSE your travelling companions won't always be of your own nationality. As often as not you'll find you've got a foreigner for company.

He or she can be any of the types described in the preceding chapter, but, being foreign, will be that much more difficult to identify as such, particularly if there's a communication problem. In this respect the language barrier can often be a blessing in disguise: The Medical Bore, for instance, won't be able to inflict tales of his ailments on you if you can't understand what he's saying.

The Untypical Tourist knows that certain types of travelling companion are more likely to come from certain nations than others. The British, for instance, produce more than their fair share of xenophobes and moaners and groaners. The French are probably even bigger grousers, with their own special brand of *en avoir marr*-ism or *s'en foutr*-ism, or if they're the sophisticated type, wallowing in philosophical ennui. The Germans are more likely to be the sort who carry pocket calculators and worry about the exchange rate and getting value for money. The Italians are perhaps the most prone to suffer – from home-sickness, or an unset stomach or *mal di fegato* or from a mysterious condition known as being *nervoso*. When it comes to medical terminology, though, no-one can touch the Americans.

But generalisations aside, not even the most skilled Untypical Tourist can always pin down exactly what a particular foreigner is all about. For one thing, foreigners don't seem to have such a highly developed system as the Brits for identifying themselves by their clothes and their accents. As Churchill once said, there's no way of telling a good Russian from a bad Russian. So how exactly can you find out whether your travelling companion, who has been holding forth so knowledgeably on the merits of *nouvelle cuisine*, is really a waiter, or an international jetsetter, or merely a waiter in mufti?

Of course, we know that underneath it all, foreigners are not to be trusted, would steal the sugar out of your tea, probably beat their wives, start their children on the booze at the age of four, and generally indulge in un-English activities. But on the surface many of them seem to be perfectly normal people who are not rabidly foaming at the mouth as we've come to expect of people on the other side of the Channel.

They, in turn, may well have similar difficulties in making out exactly who *you* are, if you don't quite conform to *their* image of an Englishman – i.e. a badly-dressed eccentric with a habit of examining the contents of his handkerchief after blowing his nose; or, somewhat more flatteringly, that celebrated English type once described by a French art dealer – 'a man with a passion for horses, playing with a ball, probably one broken bone in his body and in his pocket a letter to *The Times*'.

For our part, we tend to expect all Italians to wear gondola-striped T-shirts, have a song in their hearts and a mafia membership card in their back pockets; and all Frenchmen to wear berets, smoke Gauloises, and ride around on bicycles with a string of onions around their necks.

These sort of notions are not much help, however, when you find yourself sitting next to someone as nondescript and uninteresting as yourself and who, but for the fact that he goes in for a lot of hand-shaking and cheek-kissing, you might easily have taken for a Brit.

If he were a Brit, of course, you would simply brand him as nondescript and uninteresting and carry on staring out of the window. But as he's a foreigner, most Typical Tourists fall into the trap of wanting to show they've nothing against him. So, in the interests of international brotherhood and understanding, you find yourselves making one another's acquaintance. The result is an even more boring conversation than you would have with one of the standard British travel bores. Since neither party speaks much of the other's language you will soon be reduced to exchanging the names of football teams or cigarette brands. And although both may be non-smokers and dislike football intensely, neither will want to spoil a beautiful new friendship by saying so.

But though these conversations always start out with both sides being over-polite, and singing one another's praises, they can turn nasty. The Untypical Tourist can usually recognise the danger signs – the double-edged compliments, the excessive praise for one particular feature of another country (to cover up for the fact that he can't stand most things about it, particularly the people).

The Untypical Tourist knows that in these exchanges, it's as well to take your new friend's country seriously and not to assume that his lot see anything the way you do: they almost certainly don't have quite the same view of Napoleon or Kaiser Bill as you; and they may not even realise that their children are spoiled, noisy and badly behaved. Even people who often make light of their country, like Italians and Brits, tend to get offended when other people start doing it. In fact, when people do put themselves or their country down, it's usually just an invitation to their foreign friend to say '*au contraire*' and to tell them how wonderful they are.

So however much he may look down on a country, or however much he would like to, the Untypical Tourist always follows the golden rule that in international encounters all nations profess admiration for one another.

People from the Southern parts of Europe will say how much they admire our past, our Queen, our footballers, our language, our cars, our sang froid, our blond hair.

We Northerners will in turn say how much we admire *their* past, *their* leader, *their* football, *their* language, *their* cars, *their* joie de vivre, *their* dark hair.

How clever you are, they will say. Who else could buy up their tomatoes cheap and then sell them back in tins mixed with baked beans at twenty times the price?

How clever *they* are, you will say. Who else could, from such simple and inexpensive ingredients like tomatoes and pasta, cook up such a nutritious and noble meal and serve it at twenty times the price of the basic ingredients?

Of course, it's not always a mutual admiration society. There will be occasions when you find you are not getting the Most Favoured Nation Treatment. In that event you might try asking yourself a few questions, like:

'Did your country ever invade theirs – before the tourist invasion, that is?'
'Have you recently beaten them at football?'
'Have you recently beaten up their town after losing at football?'
'Did you ask whether the local wine was sugared?'

It's when he's not getting the MFN treatment that the Typical Tourist may be inclined to cut up rough. But even in the most extreme circumstances, the Untypical Tourist will resist the temptation to criticise; and he knows enough *not* to be frank when asked those key questions: What do you think of our country? How would you like to live here?

Even under fierce interrogation, even when his hosts seem to be begging for his real opinion, he will never give way to the urge to say what he really thinks. They may lead him on by putting themselves down ('But we're so lazy, disorganised, superficial, arrogant, etc.'), and by heaping praise upon him ('But you're so organised, rich, tolerant, successful, hardworking'). But the Untypical Tourist will respond only by telling them how wrong they are. He knows that once he starts to agree, he's in trouble.

Some Typical Tourists, however, don't restrict their encounters with foreigners to chance meetings on trains, or to contacts with those 'professional locals' that we're all bound to run into (i.e. taxi-drivers, gigolos, loo-ladies and the like). These Typical Tourists come to Ouzo determined to meet 'the real people', despite the fact that all the genuine 'amateur locals' tend to keep a very low profile during the tourist season.

Nevertheless, there is at least one tavern in the town where it's possible for the really determined Typical Tourist to meet 'the real people', and not just those locals laid on specially for Typical Tourists, like Luigi the Barman, or Abdul, their Arab houseboy.

But, as the Untypical Tourist knows only too well, this sort of fraternisation is fraught with all manner of dangers. You may start out well enough with a highly satisfactory conversation about the merits of Sebastian Coe, Franz Klammer, Eddie Merckx or El Cordobes. You may then move on from there to tell one another about your respective brothers and cousins who live in other parts of the world and whose paths, you surmise, may well have crossed. And soon enough, you may even be showing one another pictures of your spouses, children and houses. People, you may both sagely conclude, are the same the whole world over.

However, if you now believe that you've established the sort of bond that permits people to say anything they like to one another, you'll be making a *big* mistake. A sure way of putting a prompt end to the beginning of this new-found friendship is now to come up with something like:

> 'Tell me, how on earth did a bunch of mountain peasants like you lot manage to get so rich?'
> 'How is it that in a poor country like yours everyone dresses as if they're in a fashion parade?'
> 'How come a nation as incompetent and disorganised managed to run an empire on which the sun never set?'

It's at this point that you will immediately cease to be a brother-for-life, or even a distinguished visitor, and revert once more to being a loathsome Typical Tourist, now being made to feel more like an illegal immigrant.

A principal cause of these misunderstandings is, of course, language. During the winter months, the Typical Tourist will proudly complete his course of evening language classes, thus enabling him to set forth for Ouzo in the summer confident in the knowledge that he can now recite flawlessly such tongue-twisters as '*precipitevolissimevolmente*' or '*si six scies scient six cyprès chaque scie scie son cyprès*'.

The Untypical Tourist knows, however, that one's capacity to pronounce '*precipitevolissimevolmente*' diminishes very rapidly the closer you get to Italy. Thus, when it comes to foreign languages, Typical and Untypical Tourists have almost reversed roles over the years. At one time it was the Untypical Tourist who would 'have a go' and the Typical Tourist who would stick, come what may, to *Loud English*. Today it's the Typical Tourists who have developed a taste for 'speaking foreign'. Armed with their phrase-books and certain key expressions like '*Donner und Blitzen*', '*tutti frutti*' and '*merde alors*', they'll do their best to convey essential ideas like postillions being struck by lightning.

Untypical Tourists, however, are aware while these foreignisms *may* just impress their friends at home, they do not really constitute enough of a repertoire to get by in Ouzo. So, *sur place*, most Untypical Tourists have found it's better to be honest and admit they don't really know the local lingo. Anyway, if most airport announcers can't pronounce a foreign language correctly, why should you be expected to? If the top linguist in Ouzo can't draft a menu in comprehensible English, how can you be expected to do any better in *his* language? Even that pioneer of mass travel, Thomas Cook, spoke barely a word of any foreign tongue, but that didn't prevent him from getting around or make him any less *willkommen*, *bienvenu* or *benvenuto*.

7
The Way It Was

"'I visit the regulation gallery, moon around the regulation cathedral, do the worn-out round of the regulation sights yet? Excuse me!"
"Well, what do you do then?"
"Do? I flit – and flit – for I am ever on the wing – but I avoid the herds'"

Mark Twain, *A Tramp Abroad*

SO FAR we've proceeded on the assumption that, Typical or Untypical, everyone's a tourist now. But from time to time, you will come across the odd type who doesn't quite fit into this general pattern, or, at least, who tries his damnedst not to. These people don't exhibit any of the normal tourist characteristics. They don't wear funny hats; they don't carry a camera; and they wouldn't be seen dead asking the way. The point they are trying to make it that they are not Tourists, like the rest of us, but Travellers.

You can usually identify them by their well-scuffed leather luggage and old-fashioned canvas grips. You find them sitting in corner seats in trains and cafés, often reading a local newspaper or a book. (They often see themselves as the literary type.) Needless to say, the book they are reading will not be a guidebook, at least not one published in the last twenty years. These people have no need for guidebooks.

You might think from their unassuming behaviour that they're trying to go unnoticed or pass themselves off as locals. Not quite. Certainly they want to give the impression they feel at home – what globetrotter doesn't? But though their luggage may not be plastered with labels and stickers, testifying to all the places they've visited, and indicating which airlines had the privilege of taking them there, they, too, have their ways of making it clear they've been around. It usually isn't long before your attention is drawn to that remnant of a baggage stub (on which can just be made out the name of some suitably exotic destination), or some peeling steamship sticker, or Grand Hotel label.

The Typical Tourist will assume that these labels were probably stuck on the suitcase by some annoying flunkey when the owner's back was turned and which he's never bothered to remove. In fact, as the Untypical Tourist knows, they will have been put in place with extreme care, probably recently, after having been left out in the sun to fade so as to achieve just the right effect.

These people have been everywhere, but *never*, of course, on holiday. They spent a bit of time there once, or lived there for a while ('the only way to get to know a place really'). But it will always have been a long time ago, under the *ancien régime*, before all the changes, when old Trumpington-Smythe was ambassador and used to graze his polo ponies on the lawn of the President's Palace.

When our Traditional Traveller can be drawn into conversation (and he usually can), it'll generally be to reminisce fondly about the way it was – before the developers moved in, when you still got 120,000 pesos for your pound, which in those days (and he's going back a bit now) would still buy you a four-course meal and leave you enough change for a packet of cigarettes, a shoe-shine and a newspaper.

That is, of course, when the locals could be persuaded to take your money. In those days their hospitality was embarrassing. They'd be offended if you offered them cash. Not like now when they'll almost grab a tip out of your hand. You really should have known Ouzo-la-mer then. It was a different place altogether.

The big change came when they built the motorway, or the airport (i.e. before people like *you* started coming), and when they built the huge barracks of a hotel down by the beach (where *you're* probably staying). In the old days you could only get to the village by mule, banana boat or on the once-monthly post-bus. And there was only the one hotel, if you could call it a hotel – somehow it always felt more like staying with friends than being in a hotel; they always gave you the same room, with the big balcony, overlooking the bay.

The hotel's long gone now, of course, and that cosy little restaurant next door, where you used to wander in through the kitchen to see what was cooking, and where they always used to keep the corner table for you. Nothing half as drinkable in the village now as their house red – amazing little *vino* and only half a peso a litre. Produced by a little old chap up in the hills who's long since sold out to one of the big operators.

Not that the Traditional Traveller will spend all his time talking about how things were and where he's been. He'll also take a polite interest in *your* activities. After all, this mass tourism business is a bit of a new one on him. So it's rather interesting for someone like him to meet someone like you. He'll make you feel a bit like the chap in the ranks when the Duke of Edinburgh stops to talk to him. ('So you're with one of these travel companies, are you?')

He may even profess a certain admiration for you. After all, he's not sure he could take it, being herded around like that. Is it true, he will ask, that they've even got sleep-on-board buses now where everyone has a little cubicle to bunk in? Amazing.

Still, he'll concede grandly, tours are probably jolly good value. And if you've only got two weeks to spare it's probably not a bad idea to let someone organise you. He could do with a bit of organising himself, he'll admit jovially. Not long, though, two weeks, is it? Not really long enough to get to know a place properly.

This is the point where the Untypical Tourist is on his guard. He does not, like the Typical Tourist, proceed at this stage to reel off an enthusiastic account of all the things he's been dragging himself around to look at. This is precisely what his well-travelled interlocutor wants – so that *he* can then explain that *he*, of course, doesn't sightsee, at least not anymore. 'Tell me, what's it like now?' the Traditional Traveller will say, 'Can't remember when I was there last. I hear they did it up a few years ago.'

The sting in the tail for the unsuspecting Typical Tourist will be when the Traditional Traveller asks him what he thought of the little Lady-chapel tucked away in the woods; or the Pietrangeli *Madonna* that they thought for years was a Botticelli; or the pistachio-flavoured *cassata* in the little *gelateria* by the river. The Typical Tourist will then have to confess, somewhat lamely, that he missed it, or that it's a little pleasure he's saving up for next time.

Even on those occasions when the Typical Tourist feels he's done somewhere absolutely according to the guidebook, with not a sight left unseen, you can be sure that your Traditional Traveller will always manage to come up with something like: 'Yes, magnificent, isn't it? But have you seen it by moonlight?'

So, on the whole it's as well to be a bit wary of the Traditional Traveller. He feeds off other tourists – typical or otherwise. He may look the picture of innocence, sitting there in the corner reading his tome. But all he's waiting for is for someone to pop that standard travel conversation question 'Where you from?' and he'll be off and running.

It'll start with the raised eyebrow, the faint smile, the look of surprise at being addressed by a mere tourist. But it won't take him long to get into his stride, recounting where he's been and how it was before the rest of the world happened along.

And don't expect an answer to that question about his place of origin. Where he's from is neither here nor there. The Traditional Traveller is from everywhere and nowhere, and prefers to be a bit mysterious about the colour of his passport. His has been a life on the move, especially these days, as he tries to stay ahead of the advancing tourist hordes, and gets forced deeper and deeper into the backwoods in the process. He's a bit of a vanishing breed really. In fact you're rather lucky to have met him. But don't worry – as long as there are tourists there'll be travellers around to tell them tales.

8
Travellers' Tales

'A traveller has a right to relate and embellish his adventures as he pleases, and it is very impolite to refuse that deference and applause they deserve'

Rudolf Erich Raspe, *Baron Munchhausen's Narrative of his Marvellous Travels and Campaigns in Russia*

PERHAPS THE most important skill the would-be Untypical Tourist has to master is that of travel talk. For this is how you and your travelling companions will keep yourselves amused most of the time – chatting about the weather, the locals, their driving, their food, your suffering and so on.

On the whole the locals never seem to come very well out of these discussions. Some tourists may profess to admire them. Some (not many) will refrain from passing judgement. But most will be only too ready to criticise their hosts for their laziness (or hyper-efficiency), personal hygiene, sexual habits, treatment of animals and the way they bring up their children.

The Untypical Tourist, of course, knows how to slang the natives with the best of them. But as a rule he doesn't go in for the Typical Tourist's unflattering generalisations about the locals, or accounts of agonies undergone at the hands of the enemy.

The Untypical Tourist is, in practice, more likely to show a certain sympathy for the locality and the ravages *it* has suffered at the hands of the Typical Tourist – almost, in fact, the sort of line that our Traditional Traveller might adopt.

The Untypical Tourist also tries to avoid getting too carried away by his own stories – in contrast to most Typical Tourists, who would be more than a match for Baron Munchhausen himself. In fairness, of course, they need to be. The good Baron probably didn't even need to exaggerate much; travel was hairy enough in those days and didn't need much embellishment. You could just tell it like it was – give or take a few mermaids.

But now we *all* travel (which, for one thing, means we have to spend as much time listening as telling). So many tourists feel their tales have to have that something extra if they're going to make an impact.

It's in search for this something extra that people are going further and further afield for their holidays, to the remoter parts of the globe, whence they can return to tell us how it was Purgatory or how it was Paradise. More often than not, of course, it will have been Purgatory, and most Typical Tourists lay it on with a trowel as they recount how 'absolutely awful' it was.

Competing with these accounts is not always easy. And the Untypical Tourist often finds himself descending to some rather basic one-upmanship (against his better nature, and purely in self-defence, of course) in order to keep up with the opposition.

His most common gambit is to claim to have done it all 'long before'. He knows that, however far afield the Typical Tourist travels, he will have been treading a pretty well-worn path. (Even the slopes of Everest are littered with the rubbish and debris of previous excursions.) So the Untypical Tourist is usually on fairly safe ground when he claims to have been beating a particular track well before anyone else was beating it – when he had to use his ice-axe to get up a rock face, rather than to clear away the high-altitude litter.

So, the Typical Tourist didn't exactly have a ball in Ouzo this summer?

Well, the Untypical Tourist was there in '54 – biked down and bunked on the beach. There were no hotels in those days. The only place you could get a bed for the night was the local brothel and she was usually booked up.

So the Typical Tourist remembers flying into Serbia during the war? Flew in? Well, the Untypical Tourist parachuted in.

So, the Typical Tourist's worst landing was when he went on holiday to Torremolinos? Yes, the Untypical Tourist knows Malaga airport well. But has the Typical Tourist ever flown into Oudjamendougou? More or less a crater surrounded by mountains? The Untypical Tourist did it once. Never again. Night landing, force ten blowing, radar and navigational aids on the blink, one engine down, ground control couldn't speak English, no approach lighting, and they'd only managed to clear snow off part of the runway.

But 'I did it Before' or 'I did it Rougher' snobbery are far from being the only forms of travel one-upmanship the Untypical Tourist must master. There's also 'I did it with more style'.

So, the Typical Tourist always makes a point of staying in Hemingway's old room at the Palace when in Madrid? Well, the Untypical Tourist usually manages to get into Scott and Zelda's favourite room at the Ritz.

So, the Typical Tourist's favourite haunt in Paris is, like Sartre and Simone's, the Deux Magots, or perhaps the Brasserie Lipp? Well, the Untypical Tourist prefers trendy Julien's or the Vaudeville where you can see who's who *today* rather than who was who yesterday.

What most of these gambits amount to is: 'I know the place better'. The Untypical Tourist must always be in a position to give advice – even if he's only gleaned the information minutes before from the guidebook. He's the one with tips about restaurants and hotels (not that *he* usually stays in a hotel – *he* usually stays with friends):

'Try the Bonbouffe – it's not as good as when André was chef but they still do some things that are worth nibbling.'

'Stay at the Cheraton. It's so handy for Fauchon's. But only if you can get a room on the river side. If not you'd do as well – and save yourself a few francs – at a little *pension* I know, The Pas Cher du Tout.'

'If you do have time to get out of Ouzo, go down the coast to Bouzo, and make sure you stop by Harry's Bar and have one of his Bouzo Specials. And while you're there say hello to Tom and Dick for me.'

None of these places, of course, are quite what they were when the Untypical Tourist knew them. Things have changed a lot. But Ouzo's still a wonderful city, when you know your way around. It's a pity his travelling companions can't spend a bit longer there.

The Untypical Tourist is also very likely to have been in Ouzo when something very special happened. He was there on the day of the attempted coup, when the King came and ordered a Pepsi Cola at the hotel bar, when El Cordobes won six ears and three tails, when the Russians invaded.

Of course, the Untypical Tourist always knows better than to try to outdo his fellow travellers with the same kind of travel talk they're using to try to outdo him. He doesn't believe in trying to beat people at their own game.

If, for instance, the Untypical Tourist is up against the sort of travel snobs who are always being invited to dinner by the ambassador or the mayor, or going off to the theatre in a language they don't understand, he makes clear that's exactly what he came to Ouzo to avoid. Diplomatic chit-chat is all very well, but he gets enough of that at home. He came to Ouzo to get to know the people, the regular folk. In fact, the baker round the corner has invited him for lunch tomorrow. And afterwards, instead of joining the rest of the tourists at the bullfight, or the smart set at the opera, he'll be going to a football match with some of the locals, to see how *they* enjoy themselves.

This is really a form of 'The Locals Love Me' snobbery, popular with people who've been returning to the same place year after year. Their talk is all about how the locals are clamouring to take them out, heaping gifts upon them, asking their advice, inviting them back to their homes and generally laying out the red carpet.

One response to this sort of thing is 'They All Hate Me' snobbery, very popular with xenophobes. Their speciality is talking about how awful the locals are, how they were made to open every bag at the customs and how they've been getting ripped off. Or at least, how the locals have been *trying* to rip them off. But the xenophobe gives as good as he gets. He knows the natives' little games – should do after all these years.

However skilled he may be, the Untypical Tourist won't always, of course, be able to use the 'old hand' approach. At times he won't be able to conceal from his companions that he, too, is a first-timer. In this instance, therefore, he'll tend to have to rely, very crudely, on simply going one better.

So, his companions found a part of the beach which wasn't quite so crowded? Well, the Untypical Tourist just went up the coast a way and found a secluded little cove with not a soul there.

So, his companions went to the restaurant recommended in the guidebook? Well, the Untypical Tourist stumbled on this marvellous little family-run place, in one of the backstreets, superb cooking, only ten francs for the four of you, just locals there really. In fact they didn't seem to know what a tourist was.

So, his companions changed money at the bank on the corner? Well, the Untypical Tourist found this little exchange office hidden away at the back of the souk where they charge 0.5% less commission.

So, his companions went on the bus trip to Obergargl? Well, the Untypical Tourist hired a car which meant he could go on from Obergargl to Hochgargl where the view really *was* fantastic.

So, his companions had a great time at the nightclub? Well, so did the Untypical Tourist. But it's a pity they left at 2.30. It was around 3 that it really started to swing.

You can even go one better in matters of suffering.

So, your companions were delayed five hours? Well, you were delayed ten hours. So, it was a sweltering twenty-seven degrees on the coast? Well, inland on your excursion to the central plateau the thermometer was pushing thirty-seven degrees and climbing. So, your friend found a little grub in his salad? That nothing – you found a cockroach waiting for you when you got to the bottom of your lasagne.

Above all, the practised Untypical Tourist is flexible. He can go one better in any number of different directions in order to outsnob the other fellow's snobbery. He knows that at different times 'I've got more stickers on my suitcase' or 'I've got no stickers on my suitcase' can both be winners. It's the same with 'I've got real leather luggage' or 'I prefer plastic throwaway'. Or with 'My hat shouts the loudest' or 'I don't wear a hat as it makes you look like a tourist'.

'How much did you pay' snobbery also works both ways: you paid £900 – and it was worth it not to have to travel en masse and to have the extra leg-room on the plane; or you went Sunfun – and paid £700 for the same flight and for staying at exactly the same hotel; or you flew standby to Frankfurt, caught the overnight sleeper, and by taking a room without a bidet ended up paying only £350 for the whole trip.

It's the same with sightseeing. You can score by visiting everything possible. Or you can score by not visiting anything at all. Given the choice, however, the Untypical Tourist will favour the latter approach:

> 'Do you know, we've been in Pisa for a week now and we still haven't seen the leaning tower?'

'Do you know, I've been to Paris more times than I can remember. Yet, I've never seen the *Mona Lisa*. Isn't that something?'

This also applies to places in general. You can often score more points for *not* having been than for having been: Ouzo just doesn't sound like the sort of place you would want to visit any more. Anyway you certainly couldn't go now, on principle – not after their government decided to disband the National Symphony Orchestra or resume its arms sales to Chile.

It's not always easy for the apprentice Untypical Tourist to keep up with all this. The in-place to go this year may be the in-place *not* to go next year. Fashions in travel snobbery are notoriously fickle and it can be hard work staying up-to-date. To test your skills as a travel talker, or just to keep yourself in trim, have a go at the following quiz. There are, of course, no right answers – or, at least, none that will still be right a few months from now (though you may spot a few wrong ones).

1. Which of the following holidays would you rate most highly for originality:

   a) an expedition in search of Atlantis
   b) bear-shooting in the Caucasus
   c) living with Eskimos for a couple of months
   d) an inter-galactic space shuttle
   e) shark-wrestling on the Great Barrier Reef
   f) accompanying Thor Heyerdahl on *Ra IV*
   g) staying at home and watching telly
   h) no time to get away

2. Which of the following remarks conveys best that the Untypical Tourist knows his way around:

   a) I know someone who once went to Novosibirsk
   b) Whenever I change planes in Novosibirsk
   c) There's a wonderful little restaurant I know just outside Novosibirsk
   d) If you ever get to Novosibirsk, you must look up my half brother, Genghis

3. When asked to recommend a good Paris restaurant, would the Untypical Tourist say:

   a) There was one we quite liked but I can't remember the name
   b) I'll have a look in my good food guide
   c) Try Pierre's – just off the Rue Recondite. No stars in the Michelin – they're trying to stay out of the guidebooks. You'll have to go in the back way. Knock three times, give them my name and they should let you in
   d) I don't think I've ever had a decent meal abroad

4. When asked how he wants his llama steak cooked, would the Untypical Tourist say:

    a) I'll take it chopped raw local style – nothing like getting the taste of a place
    b) Grilled for me. I know what goes on behind those kitchen doors
    c) Rare. But bring it out here first so I can see it before you cook it

5. When the patron proposes the 'chateau-bottled Retsina' he reserves for 'special' clients, would the Untypical Tourist say:

    a) Fine – so long as it's the same price as the ordinary
    b) In for a penny, in for a pound, I say
    c) Now you're talking
    d) Sounds interesting. Perhaps you could put me in touch with the producer. It's the sort of thing that should go down a bomb in my three Greek restaurants in London

6. If the waiter sets before him some unfamiliar dish, would the Untypical Tourist say:

    a) Tastes wonderful. How's it made?
    b) Give me egg and chips any day
    c) Reminds me of when I first tried hot yak milk with grated garlic and ghee
    d) That's never what I ordered, is it?

7. When someone comments that the spaghetti really is cooked *al dente*, would the Untypical Tourist say:

    a) I didn't know he was the chef here
    b) Let's send Al our compliments
    c) Yes, it is a bit hard on the teeth, isn't it?
    d) Mmm, delicious

8. If there's a slug in his salad, would the Untypical Tourist say:

    a) Foreign muck
    b) A bit of local colour for you
    c) What's the Greek for slug?
    d) That's what I like about these places – so authentic

9. When asked his advice about a guidebook, would the Untypical Tourist say:

    a) I usually like to take a nineteenth-century Karl Baedeker or John Murray, just for fun

b) You can't go wrong with the green Michelin
c) The Berlitz pocket guide is all you need

10. If someone says 'We're taking an organised tour this year', would the Untypical Tourist say:

    a) We always go on an organised tour
    b) How could you?
    c) Jolly good value, I suppose?
    d) What is an organised tour exactly?

11. When someone says 'We're just back from Benidorm', would the Untypical Tourist say:

    a) I've always wanted to go there. What's it like?
    b) Where's that?
    c) How could you stand it?
    d) Must have been wonderful. They say July and August are the best months

12. When someone says 'We try to make the Biennale every year', would the Untypical Tourist say:

    a) Well, we try to make Cannes
    b) Don't you find there are just too many people there one knows?
    c) The Lido in August isn't my cup of tea, I'm afraid
    d) We've been going to the Tashkent film festival these last few years – my Uzbek's actually getting quite fluent now

13. When someone says 'We try to make Oberammergau every year', would the Untypical Tourist say:

    a) For King Ludwig's Run, I suppose
    b) Isn't that only every ten years?
    c) What's it like when they're not doing the Passion Play?

14. When asked 'How's your Katharevousa?' would the Untypical Tourist say:

    a) My what?
    b) It's all Greek to me
    c) Katharine and I are not that well acquainted
    d) My Katharevousa's OK but my Dimotiki is better and you should hear my classical Greek

15. When asked 'Ever flown into Back of Beyond airport?', would the Untypical Tourist say:

    a) Have you ever flown into Tu Vida en Tus Manos airport?
    b) I try to avoid it
    c) Yes, back in '52, before they tarmacked the runway, in a duststorm, with ground control out of action and only one engine working
    d) Only too often

9
Seeing the Sights

'Let's have a swim. I detest antiquarian twaddle'
Lord Byron

WHEN YOU'VE got there, settled in and found some friends, it's a question of how to fill those glorious fun-packed days that lie ahead.

This is usually no problem. The locals will ensure that there's plenty to keep you busy. Simply to qualify as a holiday resort a town has to lay on a certain number of tourist activities and attractions. And every Typical Tourist who wants to do the job properly will be expected to visit a certain quota of monuments, museums, beaches, nightclubs, restaurants, bars, etc.

The problem for the Untypical Tourist is how to avoid being continually shunted from pillar to post in this way. He'll probably feel that he has quite enough on his plate with all those other activities that keep tourists occupied – washing (hair, clothes, body), traffic-dodging, souvenir and clothes buying (particularly hats), money-changing, getting ill, recovering and lounging about in cafés.

There's also all that bureaucracy to attend to – buying and writing and sending postcards, taking photographs, and swapping addresses with other tourists. (But at least this is easier than it used to be in the old days when every traveller used to have to keep a detailed diary and make sketches, recording his or her 'impressions' of abroad.)

Another bureaucratic chore is filling in forms for the locals, thus giving the more imaginative Typical Tourist the chance to fill in their name as 'F. Sinatra' or 'M. Mouse', and give their sex as 'Yes Please', and object of visit as 'suntan' or 'sex'.

Some Typical Tourists, of course, really go to town with the paperwork – making a record of photos taken, at what exposure, listing purchases, recording details of expenditure, events attended, places visited, and so on.

However, the main item on most Typical Tourists' agenda is very likely to be Seeing the Sights. It's certainly the way the locals prefer the tourists to spend their time. It keeps their guests out of mischief, is a good way of taking more money off them, gives them something to take pictures of besides each other, and keeps them circulating so that they are not all clogging up the beach at the same time.

At least that's the theory of it. The problem these days is that even though the tourists are spread all over town, there often aren't enough sights to go round. The locals do try to create new ones, but it usually takes a few hundred years to build up a sight's reputation and Typical Tourists prefer to stick to the Sistine Chapels rather than go to the Matchbox Museums.

As a result, the pressure on some 'Must See' sights is reaching crisis level. Everyone, it seems, has to check out the *Mona Lisa*, take home their little piece of the Parthenon, carve their name (or Kilroy's) on Knossos. However long the queue at any given sight, there'll always be more shuffling rubber-neckers ready to tack themselves on to the end of it. They'll soon have to start setting rigid time-limits, or moving visitors around on conveyor belts ('no stepping off the belt'), or showing films and slides instead, or building replicas – as at Lascaux where the caves are now closed to visitors for ever but they're building a lookalike next door.

It's a good thing, therefore, that there are a few Untypical Tourists about who 'do' the sights by making a rapid study of the nearest postcard display on the first day and then spend the rest of their time on the beach, pretending they visited the castle some years before.

One advantage of being a local, incidentally, is that you are not under the obligation to visit the local wonders. In fact locals often take a pride in not doing so. ('Do you know I lived next door to the British Museum for twenty years and never went inside.')

It's certainly true that Typical Tourists do things abroad – like enthusiastically visit the local fish market at six in the morning – that they would never dream of doing at home. Not so the Untypical Tourist, who believes that once you've seen one fish market at six in the morning you've seen them all.

This tends to be his view of sights in general. One dolphinarium is much like another dolphinarium, one dungeon much like another. Thus, since most towns boast much the same sort of sights as any other town, the Untypical Tourist will frequently consider a number of them seen before he even gets there. Here's a list of the more standard *Sehenswürdigkeiten*:

The Old Town (The new town doesn't usually rank as a sight. Anyway that's probably where your hotel is)
The cathedral or church (including crypt, tower, side-chapels, etc., if you want to 'do' it properly)
The site of local miracle and chapel dedicated to Our Lady of Ouzo
The castle (with or without dungeon)
The artists' quarter (with or without artists)
The aquarium (with or without dolphins)
The market (can be general or specialised, i.e. meat, fruit, flea, antique, flower, stamp, bird, etc.)
The ruins (generally Roman)
The *son-et-lumière* (the ruins at night)
The smallest house in town
The oldest house in town
The oldest boozer (person or pub)

The rich man's house (can only be viewed from a distance and fleetingly as buses are not allowed to stop in front)
The house where a famous man was born, lived, died or even just spent the night (complete with manuscripts, letters to his mistress, pairs of his old boots and knickerbockers)
The bed where someone like Napoleon or Queen Victoria slept (or failing that, the chair where they sat, the spot where they stood)
The museum (mainly ancient pottery)
The folk museum (mainly potting wheels, potting clothes and potting sheds)
The art gallery (either public, with entrance fee, and paintings not for sale; or commercial, with no entrance fee, and paintings for sale)
The nightlife district (anything from a couple of seedy bars to a major red-light industry)
The booze-makers (brewery, vineyard or distillery, complete with 'tasting opportunity')
The waterside (harbour, sea, lake, river, canal – complete with boat trips)

There will also be assorted monuments, parks, gardens, cemeteries, statues, follies, grottoes, gates, belvederes, and *points panoramiques* (usually complete with an inscription from someone famous, often Goethe, saying this was the most wonderful place he had ever visited).

There will also, of course, be plenty of squares with their cafés, fountains and pigeons where you will spend a good deal of your time. Sitting about in cafés watching other people stroll past is an activity favoured by both Typical and Untypical Tourists. In fact it is almost as popular as strolling about watching other people sitting around in cafés.

Every town claims to have plenty to see. Even the most nondescript village in France will have a *'Bienvenu'* sign outside saying something like: 'La Roche-sur-Ouze – ses musées, ses ruines, ses jardins, son église, ses vins!'

But some places do have more sights than others. So sometimes when a place is a bit low on sights, the locals will create some. That's why you find specialised collection museums – of waxworks, playing cards, matchboxes, cigarette packets, pipes, engines, bottle tops, etc.

It's also fairly easy to rig up some little 'factory' – making glass, cheese, liquor, dolls, lace, carpets, pottery or whatever. It should be staffed by locals in folksy costume and also offer a demonstration (such as glass-blowing). These places are usually money-spinners as people think they are getting things at 'factory' prices. The Untypical Tourist, of course, avoids these at all costs (costs being the operative word).

One thing that every Tourist Town is sure to have is a highest point (not necessarily all that high – but anyway a highest point). It could be a hill, mountain, steeple, water-tower, monument, radio-mast, lighthouse or almost any tall building. Typical

Tourists will always be invited to go up it – by lift, cable-car or foot. If they walk, normally up a spiral staircase, they will be expected to count the steps and will frequently bump their heads on the way, despite all the warning notices. At the top they will usually find an observation deck and maybe a café or restaurant (perhaps even a revolving one).

There are different ways of doing the sights – walking tours, bus tours, in-the-footsteps tours, by-night tours. But the Untypical Tourist will usually prefer an on-his-own tour, equipped with book and map, perhaps stopping occasionally to eavesdrop on a lecture being given by someone else's tour guide.

This system usually enables him to take a few short-cuts, and to concentrate on acquiring some postcard, poster, book, or other souvenir. For the important thing is not so much seeing the sight as bringing back proof that you've seen it. This is why at art galleries and museums you see far more people buying slides and replicas of the exhibits than actually looking at the exhibits. Thus people are concentrated either in the sales area, or in the tea-room, or in the lavatories (or rather *outside* the lavatories, either queueing or trying to remember the difference between Signori and Signore, or to work out which drawing is supposed to be a little girl and which a little boy.

Don't imagine that it'll be enough to come back with just your impressions and some information. For one thing, you'll never remember much information. Stop the first ten people coming out of Westminster Abbey and ask them who built it. They won't be able to tell you – even though someone inside has just told them.

The problem is that once you've been on the tourist trail a while, sights seem more and more the same. Facts and figures blur into one another. Not so surprising since the same sort of things seemed to happen at some time or other in most places. They all built churches, won wars, lost wars, and had Empires (everyone seems to have had the dubious privilege of running the world at some stage or other).

The more towers you go up, the less likely you are to remember the exact height and number of steps to the top of any particular one. There are just too many figures bandied around by tour guides – often to add a specious authenticity to their claims. Thus you learn that today's crypt, 19.5 metres across, was the widest, but one, in twelfth-century Christendom and that four painters worked for twenty-five years (from 1128 to 1153) to complete the ceiling and the 20 metre high west wall (the second tallest crypt wall in Western Moronia) and that the floor mosaic, the best example of the work of Gianbattista Figliovic (1112–1167) is composed of 279,342 separate pieces.

Quite why any tourist should be expected to take such an interest in something that happened in another country eight hundred years ago is not clear. It does, however, give the Typical Tourist something to do, and the locals something to tell him. And many Typical Tourists do seem to feel that this sort of thing is good for them (not that they'd watch it if it was on telly, mind).

Many Untypical Tourists, however, feel you can have enough of altar-pieces and

PYTHAGAROS
CITY
PARATHANIOKOS
UNITED
FRITZ

waxworks and opt for the alternative of Get-to-Know-the-People tourism. The line here is that you didn't come to Ouzo to find out how it was eight hundred years ago, you came to find out how it is *now*. So you ride the local tram or bus, go to the supermarket, the hairdresser, the department store, the grocer – all the things, in fact, that you would normally do at home, except that in Ouzo you're really on a fact-finding mission. With a bit of practice, the Untypical Tourist can make all this sound quite plausible.

This should not be confused with the sort of *official* Get-to-Know-Modern-Moronia tourism that's offered in East European countries. Their idea of showing you how the people live is visits to factories, power plants and agricultural cooperatives and is even more boring than proper sightseeing.

Watch out, though. The tourist industry is beginning to try to cater for the Untypical Tourist drop-outs. Some places are now offering tours of the local morgue, the sewers, the kitchens of big hotels, backstage at the opera or visits to auctions, Parliaments in session, courts, etc. The locals do feel this obligation to try to keep even the Untypical Tourists busy.

One sure way of avoiding sightseeing, though, is to go somewhere during Festival time – whether it be the Festival of the Dead Rat, the Festival of the Cats, or the Festival of the Holy Blood (all these actually exist – in the same country). Being somewhere during festival time seems to excuse you from doing any proper sightseeing – partly because the locals are too busy dressing up and manning floats to take you round the town. If anyone asks you what you've been doing, you just smile and say you're there for the festival (even if not necessarily spending much time at the festival). That will usually satisfy them.

10
Tour Guides

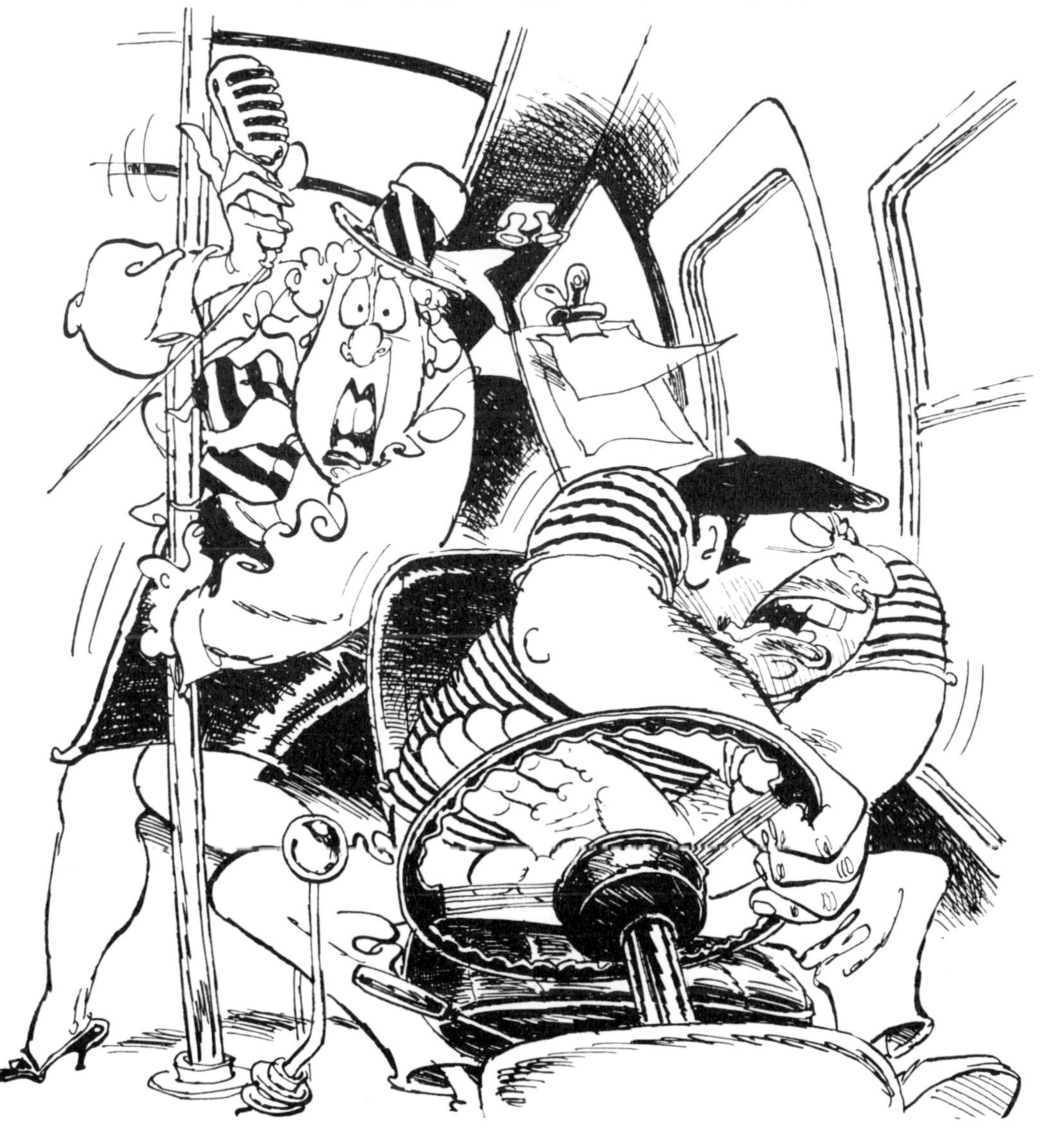

'Certain persons in Rome who get their living only by leading strangers about to see the city'
John Evelyn, *Diary*

HOWEVER MUCH of an individualist you are, however untypical a tourist, you will, from time to time, find yourself seeing the sights in the company of a group of other tourists. This invariably means falling into the clutches of a tour guide.

The guide is often thrown in, along with a lot of other unwanted extras (traditional greeting, free canvas travel bag, welcome drink, get-acquainted briefing, excursions, bonus discount coupons and souvenir book) when you go on a package holiday.

Sometimes – for instance when you've only got twenty-four hours somewhere – taking a guided tour can seem like a good idea. On other occasions you'll wind up with a guide simply because the tour company seems to have access to the town's only available means of transport. And there are, of course, times when they won't let you in to see a sight unless you are accompanied by a guide.

We're defining the term 'guide' quite loosely here to include the whole range of couriers, guides and reps (of both sexes) – anyone, in fact who collects together a group of people and whose job it is to boss them about and take them somewhere else – usually on a bus.

One should perhaps have a certain amount of sympathy for these people. It's not the most pleasant job in the world to have to explain to a group of angry new arrivals why they are not in the hotel that they booked, or why they're staying in the Palace annex (which is two miles from the Palace itself and rather less palatial), or why the bus was four hours late.

It's no wonder that some reps are pretty elusive people. ('Never did manage to get hold of that courier' is one of the standard Typical Tourist moans.)

There are, in fact, very few advantages to organised tours. Even though the guide will occasionally manage to get priority for his or her group, more often than not group travel will mean more waiting around, longer queues at loos, and slower service at the restaurants and bars where you stop – only too frequently – for refreshment or lunch (your guide gets a commission). The waiters at these places always seem to be lined up to greet you when you arrive but then disappear for good as soon as they've taken your order (they're presumably out back haggling with the tour guide over his or her cut).

Back on the bus there'll be more waiting when the traditional cry goes 'There's one missing' or when the driver can't be found.

The itinerary for a typical day's excursion might be as follows:

- Guide or bus arrives late (Moronian time. Ha-Ha.')
- Bus tours twenty other hotels in Ouzo picking up people who are not ready
- Guide introduces driver
- Guide tells a few bad jokes
- Bus gets stuck in traffic jam (because of late departure)
- Two-hour stop at coffee shop
- One-hour guided tour of Moronian National Monument (most of this time spent queueing or at souvenir shop)
- Two-hour lunch stop
- Late departure
- Traffic jam again (because of late departure)
- One-hour detour to visit doll 'factory' (where guide gets his best commission of the day)
- One-hour booze stop (perhaps where they actually make the stuff in which case it's called a 'tasting')
- Sing-song (led by guide)
- More bad jokes
- Guide passes hat round for self and driver
- Arrive back late for dinner

As well as organising you, giving instructions to the driver, handling various bits of bureaucracy (buying tickets, etc.) and collecting commissions, your guide will probably consider it his or her job to talk to you and entertain you (not always easy if you don't speak the same language, which is frequently the case).

Some guides will also see it as their job to answer questions and will happily offer additional information. Others, however, stick strictly to their well-rehearsed spiel and fairy stories. And they will take considerable exception to the enthusiastic kind of tourist who wants to know about the rate of inflation, what people earn, how they heat their homes, house prices, and how many children they have, instead of the guide's usual story about John the Blind and Moronia's rich cultural heritage.

At times one sympathises. Your fellow tourists can be a bit of a pain. Some tour guides will respond with the cheery smile-through-the-teeth approach, making light of all difficulties and hardships and playing the role of the cheery native: 'My name is Yaknowitally Manipolatolos, but call me Yak. Excuse for my English. Some little problems, yes. But this Moronia (Moronian time, not English time). Take easy. You holidays. Yak working. Take care everything'.

These sort of guides do their best to be friendly, trying to learn people's names, telling jokes (often at the driver's expense – 'and he drives even better when he's got his eyes open') and organising sing-songs. The problem is that they tend to expect some sort of audience response when they ask daft questions like 'Everybody happy?'

At the other extreme you have the no-nonsense, dictatorial types (woe betide you if you don't laugh at the jokes or if they catch you dozing off). These are the ones who say 'I'm only going to tell you this once' and make you feel as if you're back in the fourth form.

There is, of course, never much point in listening, since you'll never remember any of it afterwards. Even apparently vital information, like when the bus leaves, is irrelevant since the bus will never leave on time.

Most Typical Tourists, however, are fairly cooperative, do as they're told, laugh at the jokes, call the guide by his or her Christian name and generally let themselves be pushed around. But there are a growing number of Untypical Tourists about, who aren't always prepared to let the guide have it all his own way.

To find out if you are the ideal tourist, or if you're the type the guide would rather not have on board, try answering the following questions:

1. If the guide's explanation differs from what it says in your guidebook, do you:

    a) Snort and say 'Pah!' or 'Pfui!'
    b) Call out 'That's not what it says here, mate'
    c) Say quietly 'He's doing his best'
    d) Say nothing
    e) Turn around and say loudly 'Believe that and you'll believe anything'

2. If the guide asks if you can hear him at the back, do you:

    a) Chorus 'Yes'
    b) Remark drily 'Unfortunately'
    c) Say 'Turn it down a bit, old son, I'm trying to sleep'

3. When the guide tries to start a sing-song, do you:

    a) Join in half-heartedly
    b) Join in enthusiastically
    c) Lead the singing
    d) Say 'Not so loud, I can't hear myself think'
    e) Start a rival group singing carols or 'Yellow Submarine'

4. When the guide goes through his historical spiel, do you:

    a) Ostentatiously ignore him and carry on reading your paper
    b) Shush anyone making a noise at the back
    c) Listen attentively and ask lots of questions
    d) Not listen but occasionally murmur 'How interesting'
    e) Say 'And to think I paid good money to have to listen to this twaddle'

5. Do you:

    a) Believe everything your tour guide tells you
    b) Question everything your tour guide tells you
    c) Question out loud everything your tour guide tells you
    d) Never listen to anything he says

6. If the guide tries to interrupt the conversation you are having with your neighbour by saying 'Your attention please' or 'I'm only going to say this once', do you:

    a) Wince and fall silent
    b) Say 'Sorry, Yak'
    c) Carry on chatting
    d) Give him a V-sign
    e) Say 'I'll thank you not to talk when I'm talking, mate'

7. Do you:

    a) Make a point of never buying in any of the shops he recommends
    b) Warn all the others against buying in any shop he recommends
    c) Always buy in the shop he recommends at the 'special discount factory price'
    d) Shop where he suggests and always ask his advice before buying anything ('Do you like it, Yak?')

8. When the guide announces you have one hour of 'free' time, do you:

    a) Say 'Thank God for that' and scamper out of the bus as fast as you can go
    b) Feel lost and ask Yak's advice about where to go
    c) Ask him if you'll be safe on your own
    d) Ask him jovially if he trusts you on your own
    e) Make a point of staying away for 1½ hours

9. If the guide tells an old joke, do you:
    a) Laugh politely
    b) Laugh raucously and get the others to laugh too
    c) Say 'Have another go, mate. We all want a good laugh'
    d) Say sarcastically 'That's a good one. Haven't heard that one today, yet'
    e) Say 'Tell us when to laugh will you, Yak'
    f) Say 'Could you repeat that please'

10. If you don't feel the guide is up to the mark, do you:
    a) Give him a tip, no matter what
    b) Tell him afterwards 'If you'd played your cards right there might have been fifty pence in this for you'
    c) Report him
    d) Overtip in embarrassment, to make up for the others

11. If you ask him to make a pi-pi stop and he refuses, do you:
    a) Go meekly back to your seat
    b) Ask if anyone else wants to make a pi-pi stop
    c) Call out to the others 'Yak here says no more pi-pi stops till we get somewhere that gives him a commission. We'll now take a vote on that'
    d) Tell him 'If you don't stop I'll pee out of your window'
    e) Address yourself directly to the driver and tell him to stop the bus immediately

12. When the bus stops for drinks near a very crowded café recommended by the guide, do you:
    a) Charge out and elbow your way to the front of the queue
    b) Say 'Why can't we stop somewhere else?'
    c) Get out and meekly join the queue
    d) Go to another bar up the road
    e) Stay in the bus and moan
    f) Say to Yak 'I'll slip you a fiver if you put my order in for me'

13. When getting out of the bus, do you:
    a) Let him help you down
    b) Say 'I'm not senile yet, you know'
    c) Say 'Where would we be without you, Yak'
    d) Jump out fast so he can't touch you

14. Do you:

    a) Regard him as one of the natives
    b) Regard him as one of you
    c) Regard him as the 'man in the middle'
    d) Believe that underneath his cheerful visage, he hates all foreigners, especially Brits
    e) Believe he'd really rather be an Englishman

11
Eating Out

'Past the teeth. Past the gums. Look out stomach. Here she comes'

US army saying

ANOTHER ACTIVITY which will take up a good deal of the tourist's time will be eating and drinking in cafés and restaurants.

Unfortunately dining out abroad is not what it was. It used to be one of the best ways of really getting to grips with a country. After all, a man is what he eats and a nation is often judged by its cooking. However, genuine local cooking (what the *costa*-monger might call 'foreign muck') is becoming increasingly hard to find and is being replaced by something much more acceptable to the *costa*-monger. There's a move towards a sort of Common International Tourist Menu featuring standard items from a variety of different countries – such as pizza, chop suey, curry, hamburgers, crêpes, frankfurters, pasta and ice-cream – all, of course, served with chips and washed down with cola. As you might expect, the British, long acknowledged to be among the world's leading experts in awful food have contributed some of their own specialities like 'Hem and ekks' and cellophane-wrapped sandwiches.

One of the pleasures of eating out also used to be the contact with the locals – the waiter, your fellow diners. But that too is much reduced by the New International Tourist Menu which consists largely of so-called 'fast' foods which can be consumed on the run and so minimise any personal contact.

On occasion, however, even the most hardened *costa*-monger will get fed up with his pizza and pasta, curry and two veg, or *calamares* and chips and will be tempted to have a stab of even his fork at some of your authentic, foreign rubbish. In fact, the *costa*-monger is probably more often put off by the language of foreign nosh ('Perhaps a little *Aiguillette de Caille et Foie Gras à l'Huile de Truffe* to start, sir') than by the nosh itself. Of course, you get the same problem this side of the channel, too – with sirloin steaks being called *entrecôtes*, broth *consommé*, pancakes *crêpes*, cake *gâteau* and brandy a *digestif*.

Nevertheless many Typical Tourists do appreciate that one of the great delights of travel is a good scoff at a decent restaurant and they will duly make their pilgrimage to Ouzo's version of La Pyramide, tuck their napkin into their collar, and prepare to worship the local equivalents of Escoffier and Bocuse.

The Untypical Tourist knows, however, that unfortunately things won't always work out quite as well as was hoped. First of all, there'll probably be a lot of agonising over where to go. One of the most familiar holiday sights is a gang of tourists on the pavement outside a restaurant, trying to peek through the window, sniffing, and anxiously studying the menu to try to come to some sort of decision.

Not that you'll ever learn much about what's really going to happen to you inside from studying the newspaper reviews pasted on the window, or by sniffing at the smell coming out of the air-vents, or from your discussions with the barker on the door, or even from the number of people inside (bad restaurants often specialise in catering for groups).

The Untypical Tourist knows that all you can really do, if you don't have a recommendation, is to find a restaurant in more or less the right price bracket and hope they can live up to their claims of *'bonne table'* or *'repas soigné'*. With a little luck it'll be the sort of place that expects its clients to return. As a rough guide, here are sketches of some of the more familiar types of eating house.

Big Name Expensive

The sort of place where you're surprised to find you're admitted and where the staff earn more than you do. You go there mainly to be able to say that you, too, have eaten at the Tour d'Or or the Coq d'Argent with its legendary reputation and impressive collection of *toques*, forks, rosettes, stars, etc. You will pay for the privilege – and, to be fair, you wouldn't really be happy unless the bill was suitably astronomical, something to put on the wall and frame. They know this and are happy to oblige, deliberately including on the twenty-page menu one or two especially expensive items which people will order precisely because they are so outrageously expensive – unless it's one of those places where they don't even put the price on the menu. The food, with sorbets between courses, will be good enough. It may even be exquisite – at their prices it should be. But the portions won't always match the size of their reputation. Top restaurants seem to dish up either very lavish portions or very modest portions – and that was true even before the *cuisine minceur* came along.

Expense Account

Not such a big name, but similar prices. Basically for people on expense accounts who need to spend as much of their firm's money as possible, to impress whoever it is they are entertaining, and to show the accounts department how much things cost these days. ('And do you know that wasn't even one of the top restaurants. Think what it would have cost if I'd taken him to Big Name Expensive'.) Don't expect the quality of the food to in any way match the price.

Nouvelle Cuisine

A bit like eating Chinese – after an hour or so you'll be hungry again. Very French. Very small portions. And no longer very *nouvelle* – although still chic. A somewhat religious atmosphere may pervade, as respectful customers pick reverently at their raw goose liver and undercooked vegetables served on very large plates. Desserts will always contain kiwi fruit. The young, or not so young, chef or proprietor will probably make an appearance and expect to be duly praised for his somewhat strange yoghourt-thickened sauces and over-exotic flavour combinations. There's no need to worship. You're paying him quite enough for what you're getting.

See-and-Be-Seen

The sort of place where the jet-set go and double-park outside. May well be recently opened and probably pricey. They make their money while they can. They're the in-place with the glitterati this year, but they may well be out next year. Tend to specialise in colourful fun foods and cocktails concocted by themselves with suitably exotic names – the sort of food that's better to look at than eat. But you don't really go there to eat – you go there to see who else is there and to let others see you.

Big Name – Come Down in the World

Was once one of the plushest eateries in town but its fortunes have been ebbing for many a day. This sort of place is often found in declining Grand Hotels, near railway stations, and in East European capitals. Characterised by tall ceilings and chandeliers which need cleaning, grimy linen tablecloths and napkins, long menus with lots of different sections, and old waiters in crumpled tuxedos who are often lame or hard of hearing, and who bring your soup with their thumb in it. Half of the prices won't be marked in on the menu and half of the items unavailable. But if you're lucky they may have a good cellar.

The Perfect Restaurant

Would probably fit in about here pricewise – if it existed, that is.

The Tourist Factory

This place operates on scale, processing food and people in large quantities almost around the clock. Even though it's a bit of a barracks, it will probably try to put itself over as 'traditional' offering 'typical' fare served up by no-nonsense waiters and waitresses done up in local costume. They are often photographed smiling, holding an armful of *Biersteins*. Prices reasonable, so often very popular with Typical Tourists, especially groups who enjoy sitting on long benches, putting their arms round each other and singing oompah songs. Like it or lump it.

The *Touristique*

Probably lures you in with its 'English spoken' or 'Visitors welcome' sign, its cheerful check tablecloths and its low-price *menu touristique*. This menu (a typical example is given below) may give the lie to its claims to speak English.

SOAP OF THE DAY
or
CRUDITIES
★ ★ ★
DREADED VEAL CUTLETS
WITH PEES AND SHIPS
or
GRILLED CHAPS WITH GRINS, BOILING POTATOES
★ ★ ★
HOT TART WITH COLD CREAM
or
CHOCOLATE MOUSE

The menu may well also include a carafe of Red from the Hose or a bottle of Pschitt to wash it all down. However, they may not be all that keen to offer you their *table d'hôte* once they get you inside, trying to palm you off first with the *à la carte* menu and making you ask for the *menu du jour*.

The Tourist Trap

Similar sort of place but even more of a con. May well have an *entraîneuse* or even the proprietor himself barking on the door to lure you in. Once inside, you are almost sure to find that the seemingly good value *prix fixe* menu advertised on the sandwich board on the pavement outside has already run out. (This can happen even as early as 12.45 p.m.)Nothing else on offer will be half as reasonable and the extras will be totally unreasonable.

Family Run

The proprietors don't just live 'over the shop'. The restaurant is more or less their home. The restaurant kitchen will be their own kitchen. One of the doors will open onto their living room from which children, cats, dogs, and grandmothers in slippers will wander in and out. There'll be a television on in the corner to entertain you while you eat. The daughter of the house will be your waitress. You'll feel you should apologise for barging in on them during lunch hour.

The Real Find

As with the perfect restaurant, there are not many of these about. But you may from time to time stumble on one somewhere up a backstreet run by a pleasant middle-aged woman who loves cooking, is not interested in money, and is full of apologies for her delightful hand-scrawled menu. Don't tell anyone.

The False Find

A hole-in-the-wall up a backstreet, seating about six, which specialises in catering for the Typical Tourist who desperately wants to make a find. From the outside this 'restaurant' may not look much different from 'the real find'. The food, however, will be awful. Don't be misled by the three or four regulars inside eating it. They're allowed to eat there free to persuade the unwary tourist that this is where the in-the-know locals go. The owners make their money out of their innocent victims.

The Tourist Special

Feeding time can be fun – or so it seems to say in the brochure. You usually book these places in advance, against your better judgement, on the strength of their publicity ('Unlimited' this and that). You pay an all-in-price for a session where you will do things like get dressed up in a peasant's smock, quaff horns of ale, eat with your fingers, be served by lads and wenches in medieval costume, and generally wassail the night away. You'll be given a scroll souvenir menu (with 'ye' in front of each item) to take home with you. Will be billed as a once-in-a-lifetime experience. Once will certainly be enough.

The Greasy Spoon

Plenty of atmosphere – tables uncleared, overflowing ashtrays, chipped glasses and cups, no soap or towels in the loo. Attracts those diners who take a pride in eating as cheaply as possible or have no choice. There'll be one menu – take it or leave it. Don't look in the kitchen on any account or you'll never be back. Not that you'll always have the chance of a return visit – he may lose his licence next time the health inspectors come around. Make sure you wipe the cutlery and your glass before you start. And don't lean on your cutlery, it'll probably bend double.

The *Romantica*

Dark table lamps or candles, heavy curtains, piped Mantovani or One Thousand Hawaiian Guitars in the background. The menu (she may get a special one without prices) will feature several dishes for two, and a number of items (particularly desserts) that the waiter can set on fire before your very eyes. There will also be one or two specially expensive items on the menu, in case he or she wants to impress. Wine list will be overloaded with very expensive wines (mark up about 300%) for the same reason. The rather smooth waiters are trained to be especially deferential to males. *Maître d'* will come over often and ask if everything is OK. They often allow in some flower-seller or student troubadour, who like these restaurants because the men overpay.

The Ethnic

Run by hairy moustachioed refugee, his hairy moustachioed wife and their daughter (also hairy and moustachioed). Decor will consist primarily of things hanging from the ceiling and walls, like sausages, onions, gourds, agricultural implements, weapons, etc. Incomprehensible menu, but a lot of the cooking will be done semi-publicly, perhaps in a corner of the room, so you can see what you're getting. Usually bring you hot peppers to munch while you're waiting. An 'excuse fingers' sort of place.

Health Food

Decor will be plainish, with the walls pine-clad, or perhaps brick, possibly painted white. Furniture will almost certainly be pine with one big table where all the bowls and pots of yoghourt, nuts, buckwheat, lentils, seaweed, quiches and granary breads will be laid out. The key word is 'whole' as in 'wholefood' or 'wholemeal'. Usually self-service, but you may be helped by proprietor and wife (who never look quite as healthy as they should) clad in their blue striped butcher's aprons. Not for the *Feinschmecker* or for people given to making comparisons with the price of beans in their local market. Suitable for those who eat to live, rather than those who *live to eat*.

* * *

Once inside a restaurant you normally have to make the best of it – though you do find people who spend an hour outside on the pavement studying the menu, eventually come in and sit down for five minutes, and then change their mind and leave, without even making their excuses.

The Untypical Tourist knows that much will depend on that all-important first encounter with the staff – waiter or waitress, or *maître d'* and Sommelier if you're somewhere posh. Your fate is very much in the hands of these people and it's important to make a good first impression.

The waiter sees it as his job to put you in your place in more ways than one. Not only will he show you to your seat, he will also have sized you up, come to a quick decision on your station in life, made you feel accordingly inferior or superior and put you in a seat that reflects that station.

If you get the table near the loo, behind the pillar, by the kitchen door, by the entrance, or by the coat rack, or if you get shunted into the side room or back room, he doesn't rate you very highly. (This is rather more likely to happen if you're dining on your own.)

Waiters and waitresses are sensitive souls, harrassed middlemen and -women constantly on the run between the frying pan in the kitchen and the fire of their clients. Their one consolation in life is that they always have the upper hand over those clients. In any conflict between diner and waiter, there's one thing you can be sure of – the diner won't win (remember all those old jokes about flies in your soup).

So the Untypical Tourist tries not to annoy his waiter. For he can wreak such terrible revenge. He has so many ways of punishing you. He can wipe the crumbs into your lap, he can *not* bring the bread, he can forget the wine, or that second beer, bring your coffee cold, or give the last House Special to someone else. He can keep you waiting for ages between orders and courses, ensure you don't get what you ordered, and show you up to other diners.

Even worse, he can flick ash in it, or spit in it, gleefully shouting to his colleagues when he returns to the kitchen: 'He ate it, you know'. (Never go into the kitchen, by the way. You may get a nasty shock.)

The basic way in which the waiter exercises mastery over you is by controlling the timing of your meal. (Remember that celebrated epitaph for a waiter: God finally caught his eye.) You attempt to alter the pace at your peril. This will merely ensure that nothing ever comes at the right time. You order an aperitif and it will arrive just as you're finishing your soup. You order another beer or bottle of wine and it will arrive just as you get to the coffee. Some courses will be piled almost on top of one another and then there'll be a long gap between others. And at the end of the evening just as you're sitting back, relaxing and telling a few stories, you suddenly find your dessert, coffee and brandy dumped on you all at once in double-quick time – a clear signal that you're overstaying your welcome. And don't assume that forward planning can do anything to revise this schedule; you may try to beat the system by booking your second round of drinks, or your coffee and brandy, well in advance, but that just means he's even more likely to forget.

Sensing that the key to it all is how they rate with the waiter, some people go to great lengths to get the waiter to revise his initial judgement of them. They self-importantly insist on a better table, start waving rolled-up notes around, snap their fingers or clap loudly for the menu, order the most expensive items and enquire knowingly about the more obscure dishes.

Waiters are only human and may well respond to a little palm-greasing or the prospect of it. But even if you do succeed in getting a better table, you will feel that, deep down, the waiter still holds to his initial judgement of you. And when he takes your order, you can almost see him smiling to himself, as if your choice of dishes confirmed exactly what he thought about you all along. Waiters are the original men who knew too much.

Your initial tussle of wills will be over the menu, a document which will be a fairly accurate reflection of the restaurant itself, or its aspirations. Menus can be grubby, curling at the edges, hand-written, printed, long, short, very big, plastic, fun, multi-sectioned, leather bound with tassels, with numbers (i.e. Chinese), oddly shaped, trick menus (full of either/or suggestions for combined dishes) or chalked on the blackboard on the wall.

It's the waiter's job to defend the menu. The Untypical Tourist knows better than to ask him if it's fresh or not, or any good. (What do you expect him to say? That it's not good? That the fresh salmon is out of a tin, that the 'veal' is actually well-disguised chicken, and that the *'tarte'* is not actually *'maison'*?) Some people try to develop a relationship with the waiter, ask his advice about dishes and wine, make him feel responsible for the success of their meal. They try to get him to abandon his official stance, to make friends with him, to get a dialogue going. Certainly this may mean holding the waiter up, but then these people, as they are at pains to make clear, are not *ordinary* clients. This will be emphasised by the little riders added after each dish is ordered ('. . . and the greens a shade underdone, if you would').

Some people try to engage the waiter's sympathy for their appreciative but sensitive stomach. They put on a perplexed 'I'm not sure that there's anything that really tempts me' expression, making the waiter feel like an insistent host. In the end they'll give way to the waiter's suggestion with an 'OK – if you really recommend them . . .'

The waiter, of course, sees through all of these performances. But if you act your part with enough flair, he will probably play along. That's his job after all.

Sometimes you'll come across less hard-pressed waiters and barmen who enjoy having a natter, and who will happily spend the day discussing the state of the world. But in these cases, it is probably best not to encourage them since it's likely to mean you'll be chatted to, rather than served.

As soon as you've placed your order, the menu will be withdrawn. It's not quite clear why waiters always insist on removing the menu quite so promptly. Do they want to get it away before you have a chance to make a note of the prices, or to notice whether it's *boisson compris, prix nets* or whatever? Or do they want to prevent it from becoming even more dog-eared, or to stop you from scribbling in it, or from laughing at some of the more entertaining formulations (hot tart of the house, etc.)? More probably it's simply another of the waiter's ways of exercising control. He is the master of the menu which he grants to you for strictly limited periods, on request.

You will not, however, be permitted to do anything without the menu, even if there only seems to be one menu in the house. Any attempt to buck the system, for instance by trying to get off to a quick start by ordering as soon as you sit down before seeing the menu (or even on your way to your table), will be to no avail. This also applies to the secondary items – dessert, cheese, wine. Nothing will be registered until you have perused and given due consideration to that document, once again. Any attempt to cheat by nobbling another waiter for the menu, or getting one from the people at the next table, or taking it from the rack yourself, will bring due retribution in time. It's a golden rule that the more you try to run your own meal, the more your waiter will insist your meal is run *his* way.

Not that the way he runs things won't be affected sometimes by matters outside his control. He may, for instance, be the only waiter for the whole restaurant, or each waiter may have twenty tables to look after, in which case he's likely to be leading a harassed life, his only respite being the quick drag on his smouldering cigarette end, as he gets inside the swing doors. In such situations there's no way that service can not be slow. Equally, there can be plenty of waiters, but only one cook, with much the same result.

This sort of thing is most likely to happen at those large outdoor cafés. The waiters at these establishments are usually bad-tempered, thin on the ground, and operating in a zone a long way from base. They thus develop a technique of dodging rapidly between tables in an effort to evade the calls of frustrated clients, all snapping their fingers, clapping their hands or tapping glasses or cups with their spoons. Of all waiters these are the masters at turning a deaf ear, at not having their eye caught, at looking at you without seeing you. Traditionally white-jacketed and black-trousered, they always arrive with a circular tray held shoulder high and packed brimful. They never remember who ordered what. Anything that ought to be hot will be cold by the time it gets to you. It's never worth trying to hand over to him personally any money for your bill; just leave the amount on your chit and beat it.

Mind you, some Typical Tourists do ask to be served badly. They come in a big group – each of them ordering a different starter, frequently changing their minds and taking the mickey and asking if they get a reduction if they don't have the side salad, or if they can swap the flan on the set menu for cheese. As soon as there's a slight delay,

ATHLETICO OUZO 0
TOTTENHAM HOTSPUR 4

one of their number will go up and bang a coin on the counter, or stick his nose into the kitchen. No wonder, therefore, that these people will often find that their table is in a sort of no man's land, not coming into any one waiter's section. The waiters will take turns at fending them off. They know in advance that there'll be no tip at the end from that sort of group – just a pile of coins and notes which they hope is the right amount, left on the table after much discussion and confusion about how to divide up the bill.

Not that the Untypical Tourist will avoid causing the waiter any bother at all. You'll get no respect for being over-compliant. Most menus do require some explanation and it's nice to know exactly what it is you're ordering.

Having placed your order, there'll be a chance to study your surroundings, criticise the music and see what they've decided to hang on the walls – ponchos, pitchforks, carriage lamps or whatever. There's also a chance to study your fellow diners, to see who else made the decision to eat there, and whether they have any objectionable habits like belching or bringing their dogs in with them. You'll be able to see if the locals are getting priority or the foreigners, and if there's contact to be made. There are restaurants where people talk to one another and restaurants where they don't. If not, you can just listen to the rumbling of tummies, play with the toothpicks, throw the bread about, make a few crumbs and wonder if it's taking a long time because he forgot your order, or because the chef is actually cooking it, and whether the prices really are reasonable or it's just that the food is frozen.

The Untypical Tourist also enjoys having fun with what many consider the ultimate challenge in a foreign restaurant – getting the waiter to bring you a glass or a jar of tap water. It's rarely easy.

At first he will probably pretend not to understand, brushing aside your request, and trying to palm you off with mineral water for which you will be overcharged or, sneakier still, bringing you tap water in a glass which he later claims was mineral water ready poured. If you persist, saying you don't want mineral water, or bottled still water, but ordinary tap water, you'll probably get the aren't-you-a-bit-of-an-oddball look, or the are-you-just-trying-to-cause-trouble stare, before he finally brings you, after much delay, a very small glass of H_2O, which will be set before you, with a look daring you to ask for another.

Anyone who succeeds in promptly getting served with a large jar of tap water and not paying extra for it usually earns a waiter's undying respect.

The reason for all this may be that restaurants make their money on extras. It goes against the grain for a waiter to bring something he can't charge for. Profits are made on the aperitif; or the mineral water; or the Grand Cru Kopfschmerz; or the beer (which will be expensive-imported rather than local unless you specify); or the post-prandial cup of coffee; or the sweet trolley; or the local firewater distilled by the monks up the road (the sort of stuff that is not too bad *sur place*, but tastes like turpentine when you take a bottle home). These are all items, of course, that you never seem to notice the price of at the start as you study the set menu.

For many, the most dramatic moment is when you finally get the bill – less so when the waiter does his adding up on your paper tablecloth, but most definitely when the waiter sidles over with that little white slip discreetly folded on a saucer, and asks rhetorically 'Hat's geschmeckt?' or 'Ça a été?' before beating a hasty retreat and leaving you to assess the damage.

Invariably, you are in for a few surprises – the substantial cover charge, perhaps, which seems a bit steep in view of the fact that you have broken nothing, have used very little in the way of bread, butter, mustard, salt and pepper, have not soiled the table linen and have no intention of walking off with the cutlery, ashtray or soap from the loo. You may discover also that you're getting charged for those nuts and other bits and pieces you didn't order that came with the aperitif and that the water you had was apparently mineral water, and that the second cup of coffee your genial host insisted on pouring was not on the house after all.

It's not often that a tourist, Typical or Untypical, is happy with his bill – much as he wants to feel he's got value for money. Sometimes he will have the satisfaction of finding something wrong with it (if he can read the waiter's deliberately illegible scrawl). Restaurants frequently make a point of building in a few deliberate mistakes – perhaps adding in the date, or charging for service twice (which, if challenged, they'll say is VAT). But usually in the end the diner will just have to pay up and shut up, perhaps crumpling up his napkin to get maximum value rather than folding it up neatly as he might have done otherwise.

At the end of the day, your biggest gripe is likely to be not the bill or the service, but the coffee. Generally speaking, in restaurants you get what you pay for: if you choose the cheapest *menu touristique* on the block don't be surprised that your cream-of-whatever soup was tinned, that the side salad consisted of three lettuce leaves and a grated carrot, that the steak was miniature rather than minute, accompanied only by a token presence of potatoes and vegetables, and followed by a tiny *crème caramel*, all washed down with a quarter of wine that would have been more at home in a vinegar bottle. The quality of the coffee, however, will never seem to bear any relation to the price you pay or the reputation of the establishment. Some exquisite meals can be followed by awful coffee and vice versa. Still, perhaps one shouldn't take it out on the coffee too much. As someone once said: 'Don't criticise the coffee: you may be old and weak yourself someday.'

12
Shopping

'It was beautiful and simple as all truly great swindles are'
O. Henry, *The Octopus Marooned*

ANOTHER MAJOR holiday pastime is shopping, finding things on which to spend those hard-earned travellers cheques. All Typical Tourists are forever engaged in a search for some 'gizmo' or other – something they don't need but have to have.

No matter that these days you can get all of these items at home, and probably better made and cheaper. These are not normally the sort of things you would want to buy at home. Anyway, the main reason you buy them is not so much because you want them, as to prove you've been away.

Of all the useless objects that clutter up your home, how many come from some *beriozka* abroad? How many bottles of unpronounceable and undrinkable foreign firewaters, brought back from various parts of the globe, are crammed into the rear of your drinks cupboard. Do you, or do any of your friends really need a leather-covered Kleenex box, or a souvenir ballpoint pen from Auschwitz or a chiming Easter egg, or a transistor radio shaped like a banana?

In a way the very appeal of some such items is their almost deliberate bad taste. It's hard to see why else anyone would buy a pair of Union Jack underpants or a pair of yellow knickers with 'Ooh you are awful' on the front and 'But I like you' on the back.

One feature of souvenir buying is the compulsion of many Typical Tourists to keep on buying the same thing. Everywhere they go they have to buy a folk-doll or a paperweight or a pipe or a penknife. When they've got more than a few (it doesn't take long) they rationalise their mania by calling these things a collection, and they even start asking other people to bring them back specimens from abroad.

Untypical Tourists have a stock of handy excuses to avoid being commissioned in this way. They know that whenever they go on holiday, someone will ask them to bring him back some object or other. It'll either be another item for his collection, or a replacement for something which originally came from abroad, but which has since got lost, broken or worn out. Your friend's parting words to you will be along the lines of 'You can get one in any old ironmongery . . .'

This will, of course, never be the case. You will spend hours and days of your precious vacation looking for this object, attempting to describe it to uncomprehending shopkeepers and, in the end, face the choice of going back and telling your friend you couldn't find it (he won't believe you looked) or getting something vaguely like it (he won't believe you tried).

Anything else but this particular object, however, you can now find just about anywhere you go abroad. As with the Common International Tourist Menu, we are now in the age of the Standard International Souvenir. You can get bullfight posters in Brighton, Carnaby Street T-shirts in Cologne, castanets in Copenhagen, model mermaids in Madrid. There is probably not a single souvenir shop anywhere in the world that does not sell Snoopy mugs. There is certainly not a tourist town anywhere that doesn't offer its visitors hand-crafted glassware, woodwork, leatherwork or basketwork. But at least this sort of *Handarbeit* does pretend to be locally made. Not so the growing range of 'drugstore' or 'petrol station' items – sunglasses, make-up, cassette players, radios, records, tennis rackets – all things that today's Typical Tourists also tend to pick up abroad, rather than buy at home.

But perhaps what we buy is less important than the ritual of shopping itself – the chance to use one's spare cash and to pit one's wits against the locals. Most of us may not possess many talents, but one thing we all think we know how to do, is shop. So most Typical Tourists need only glimpse a market, *souk* or 'discount' factory, or spot a sticker saying 'sales' or '10% off' in some foreign language, to start the adrenalin flowing.

The ritual begins with the preliminary skirmishing as they wander round the store, poker-faced (that's what they think), telling the shopkeeper they're just browsing while he encourages them to do so.

'Sure. You come in. Please. No obligations. You looking. You no want, you no buy. You English? To English I give good price. What you looking? What you want? You like? How much you pay? You tell me price. Which one you like better? You try.'

The Typical Tourist plays it all pretty cool (so he thinks), deviously working his way by the most circuitous route imaginable towards the thing he really wants. He feigns interest in various objects in that general area before piping up, oh, but oh, so casually (though his quaking voice generally gives him away): 'And what about *that little one at the back*? How much is that?' Nine times out of ten, of course, the shopkeeper knows immediately that this is what he really wants. 'Ah, *señor*,' he says, 'that, *señor*, that is something very special. You have very good taste, *señor*. I show you.'

At this point, the Typical Tourist may try to get the shopkeeper off the track again, and start asking about other items, but, in the end, they both know that the Typical Tourist will always come back to *that little one at the back*. This is the shopkeeper's chance, though, to try to increase the scale of the deal and to persuade his client to spend a lot more than he ever intended by chucking in a few extra items and offering a discount for buying in bulk. 'I tell you what I do,' he says. 'You take this and this and this and I make one price. Good price. For you.'

This is when the Typical Tourist may have a moment of uncertainty, when he may want to go away and think about it all (fearing, however, that during that time someone else may come in and walk off with *that little object at the back*, *his* little object at the back). This is when the merchant will sense the need to reassure his victim, to offer a cup of tea, to let him take the object out into the light, to let him try it on again, to tell him that his aunt really will love it, that *Lederhosen* really do suit him, that stacked up against twenty others *that little one at the back* may look ordinary enough, but that on its own on his mantelpiece at home, it will look really very special indeed.

If, at this point, the Typical Tourist begins to haggle over the price again, to look for flaws in the merchandise, to say he really didn't want it anyway, that they're cheaper up the street, that this is all the money he has, then it almost certainly means (even though he may not know it yet) that he's decided to buy it.

All that really remains to be discussed is the bureaucracy of how to get back the value added tax, purchase tax, gift tax, sales tax, or government tax or whatever (ah, the magic of those words 'tax-free') and trying to get an additional discount for cash, hard currency, or travellers cheques.

It would be wrong, however, to give the impression that every shopkeeper in a tourist resort behaves like some Middle Eastern carpet salesman, turning his shop upside down for the Typical Tourist so that he feels guilty if he goes away without buying something.

That certainly isn't the way it's done on the Rue du Faubourg St Honoré or the Via Condotti. Some European shopkeepers are very restrained. Some go to the opposite extreme, seemingly ignoring you and apparently not wanting to sell you anything. But don't be deceived. They do really. Even the most genteel of establishments are usually prepared, when it comes down to it, to *'faire un prix'*.

It's just a question of different sales techniques. There are some things that sell themselves, that Typical Tourists want precisely because they can't afford them. Here the prohibitive pricetag is one of the attractions. The Typical Tourist is in thrall to that law which says: 'The more you want something, the more it'll cost you; and the more something'll cost you, the more you want it'.

The more difficulties in your path, the more desirable the object becomes. If it's heavy, fragile, difficult to get home, complicated to ship, hard to get an export certificate for, requires much form-filling and negotiation with the proprietor over coffee in a private room, the Typical Tourist will be that much more determined to become the 'exclusive' possessor of his own amphora, carpet, 'antique', painting, sculpture, ikon or other objet d'art. (Not that he'll ever want to take it to Sotheby's, mind, for fear of being told it really isn't eighteenth-century after all.)

This is the same sort of sales psychology that's practised by the type of shopkeeper (an antique dealer, perhaps) who appears to be so much in love with his treasured objects that he doesn't want to part with them. He may strategically place one or two of them so that you knock them over and break them, but he'll virtually refuse to sell you anything. This, however, is all part of the sales technique, based on that ancient law that he who mentions a deal first loses half of the bargain. So the most you'll get out of him is a 'take it or leave it' price. He knows that the Typical Tourist will want to buy it just to prove him wrong.

In the end, everything has its price and only the savvier Untypical Tourists will evade the traps that are set for them. Take, for instance, those optimistic forays that the Bargain-hunter will make into the backstreets in search of a small shopkeeper who's having a slow day. Bargain-hunter will eventually light on some little old man up an alleyway where he'll find just the thing he's looking for. It'll probably be lying half-hidden in the clutter and grime at the back of the shop. (Little old men in backstreets are the world's greatest experts at half-hiding their choicest items in the clutter and grime at the back of their shops.) It must be a snip, thinks Bargain-hunter. And he'll also have the satisfaction of buying from a little old man in a backstreet. Many Typical Tourists derive an obscure pleasure from buying from little old men in backstreets. (The little old men know this, of course, which is why they set up their little shops in backstreets in the first place.)

This does not just apply to little shops in backstreets. Typical Tourists also enjoy buying something off a barrow, or a market stall, or from a collection spread out on the ground. They much prefer to buy a painting off the railings, from a man with a beret and with a knotted handkerchief round his neck, who says he's the artist, than from a proper art gallery.

The reason is that it's in these sort of transactions that you can feel you've made a friend as well as a purchase, where you can be persuaded that you're being offered that 'special' price because you're you and because you would find a good home for the object in question. 'Listen,' the little old man will say in a conspiratorial whisper, 'if you don't tell anyone, I make price for you . . .'

In so doing of course, he has provided the Typical Tourist with something else he wants – an experience and a tale to tell. In fact the Typical Tourist could probably have bought his joss-sticks or his poncho or his *Alpenstock* that much cheaper at the hotel souvenir shop. But then he wouldn't have had his story about the little old man and how he picked up his bargain. (The Typical Tourist won't be too specific, of course, when he tells his story in case someone begins to wonder if it actually *was* a bargain.) Typical Tourists can often pay a lot of money to get something they can *call* a bargain.

It's these tales to tell, these experiences, these memories that you can't buy at the airport or the souvenir emporium in the centre of town. These shops may well have a large stock, well displayed, at good prices. The objects will be kept polished and dusted by pleasant local girls who will smile winningly as they gift-wrap your purchase with pretty paper and a magnificently tied ribbon. But somehow many Typical Tourists would rather pay a little bit more to get it wrapped up in a bit of yellowing newspaper and handed to them by a croaking old man in a backstreet.

13
Romance

'Amor, di nostra vita ultimo inganno'
Giacomo Leopardi, *Ad Angelo Mai*

FOR MANY Typical Tourists, the romance of holidays is precisely that. Love not only makes the world go round. It's also what sends us around the world. The main reason why a lot of people go on holiday is quite simply the prospect of having a torrid affair, or failing that, of getting a sexy tan, and parading in their slinky new outfits.

Romance, or the search for it, certainly helps keep the Typical Tourist busy. There would be something incomplete about a holiday without someone to spread on your suntan lotion (or to spread suntan lotion on), to admire your all-over tan, to wander through the market with, to share exotic drinks and a straw with, and to gaze at sunrises and sunsets with.

The big question is do you take your romance along with you or do you find it *sur place*. In these progressive times, of course, some couples manage to do both. One recalls that story, much told to Typical Tourists by tour guides, about the Englishman (unless the guide has a party of Brits on board, in which case it'll be a German): The fellow has just returned from a holiday in Paris with his wife, and is telling his mates in the pub how marvellous it all was. Someone, he recalls, picked you up in the morning, showed you the sights, wined and dined you in fine style, took you out on the town in the evening and then home to bed, and when you woke up in the morning, there was always a five hundred franc note tucked under your pillow. 'And this all happened to you?' his friends ask incredulously. 'Well, not to me exactly,' he replies, 'but to my wife every day.'

Abroad may be awful but there is something about it which does seem to get the sap of the Typical Tourist rising. Perhaps that's why the more exciting sexual mores (the French way, the Greek way, the Italian way, etc.) are all thought to come from somewhere else – usually somewhere further South, as far as Northern Europeans are concerned. (The Mediterraneans of course probably get turned on by the English way or the Dutch way – well *perhaps*). Byron wasn't the only one to see the sensuous South as an escape from sexual repression. The steamy heat, those exotic juices, those pulsating rhythms, those sultry smiles all seem calculated to make the Typical Tourist lose his or her inhibitions.

Another factor may be the pressure of time. Only having two weeks or two days for those amorous escapades does concentrate the mind and make the Typical Tourist get on with it – particularly when there's not much else to do or to think about.

The language barrier also seems to be an important stimulus to sexual communication abroad. Having only limited command of a foreign tongue often forces the Typical Tourist to abandon his usual circuitous subterfuges like 'Come up and see my etchings some time', for a more direct approach like 'I want to sleep with you', or 'What about a spot of jiggy-jiggy?'

Phrases that sound corny in English like 'Is that seat taken?', 'Do you come here often?', or 'I came here to get to know the people' can represent a pinnacle of linguistic achievement in a foreign language. They will thus be proudly pronounced and are thus more likely to lead the Typical Tourist rapidly on to more intimate things than would the choice, but less obvious, expression he would have come up with in his own language.

Even those foreign names sound sexy. There's something about someone called Svetlana or Sasha. Mind you, they probably think the same about people called Doris and Bill. For us, though, Casanovas are only really credible if they have a name like Julien Sorel, or, indeed, Casanova.

There are plenty of them about, of course, in the world's bottom-pinching zones. Indeed, they are probably one of the prime tourist attractions. As we've said, romance is one of the main reasons Typical Tourists go abroad. And however much Northern maidens (or matrons, for that matter) may claim to be annoyed by the attentions of the local Kamaki ('Excuse me, Miss, where's the Eiffel Tower, Colosseum, Acropolis?'), they don't always seem to go out of their way to discourage them. They'll spend a lot of time complaining about their *pappagallo* admirers in their slip-off moccasins and painted-on shirts (they might as well have a sign on the back saying 'sex appeal – please give generously'). But, very often, one feels, the damsels do protest too much. Certainly those Latin Lotharios (a surprising number of whom claim to have studied at Oxford, Harvard or Uppsala, and to be slumming it because they got bored with their country estate) never seem to have much trouble notching up a respectable score of points in the course of a season. (No prizes for stating which nations rate the most or least points in the sexual league table for making free with their favours.)

It's all the attraction of opposites, of course. Northern women all go through their Latin lover phases, and Southern males do seem to have this thing about pale skinny Northern women.

And as we all know, those dusky Latin sexpots feel an irresistible attraction for the lanky limbs, hairless chest and somewhat less than obvious sexual ways of the average Englishman. 'Oh, Beeel,' she will swoon ecstatically as he recounts the intimate details of the transfer negotiations for Albion's lastest striker, or shows her his CAMRA membership card, explaining how the local brew is not a patch on the real ale you find back in Barnsley.

A foreign romance is certainly the best way to get to know the natives and learn the lingo – some of it, anyway. It has been said, though, that holiday romances are the reason why so many people's knowledge of a foreign language is restricted to the naughty words and key ideas like 'Shall we go to bed?' or 'My wife doesn't understand me'.

There are certainly romantic advantages to be derived from speaking a language badly. When the outrageous is said with a foreign accent it somehow seems more forgivable. You can say what you like in a language that's not your own. It doesn't really matter. Foreign languages do have this liberating effect. And it's fun saying things like *'mon chou'* which would sound ridiculous in your own language.

Romance also teaches the Typical Tourist a certain linguistic tolerance. His usual contempt for the way foreigners massacre his own language can be much curbed when the massacring is being done by a loved one. He may even discover that there is a certain charm to his language, when spoken appallingly, by someone gazing adoringly into his eyes at the same time.

It's in pursuit of romance that the Typical Tourist is most likely to sally forth to sample the local nightlife. The prospect of doing the town 'by night', of course, is an idea alive with sexual promise and possibilities – even if it's only Ouzo-la-mer by night.

Off we go with our escort, or in search of one, to some disco (probably called the King's Club) or some dive in the seamier sections of the town, offering 'first bottle champagne free' or, if it's even more of a dive, and they're not expecting you to stay long, just 'first drink free'.

If you decide, after studying the photos outside of the 'international' cabaret stars performing inside, to make the transition from tourist to punter and actually go in, you will often find that the place doesn't quite live up to your Plato's Retreat expectations. As often as not, it'll be on the seedy side, with an unctuous host in shiny tuxedo, bow tie and toupee, who keeps on wishing you welcome in several different languages (in descending order of proficiency) and inviting you to give 'a round of applause' for the resident jugglers, flamenco star or belly-dancer.

At some point, be warned, one of these performing ladies is certain to try to lure some unsuspecting male Typical Tourist on-stage. It's probably better that this person should not be you or your partner – unless you happen to have a penchant for having your shirt unbuttoned on stage by a blowsy lady who makes you perform awkward gyrations at the same time, to the general amusement of the assembled company. Actually those chaps who do comply are usually so far gone that they don't remember much about it afterwards – though no-one else in the room will ever forget it (the man will for ever after be branded as 'that chap – you know, the one with the belly-dancer'). If he's in any doubt about what his friends keep telling him happened, the nightclub photographer usually has evidence (which can be made available to all) that the events so described actually *did* take place.

In fact, it's as well to be wary of local dances in general. The Untypical Tourist knows that it's as well to stifle any inclination he might have to out-Zorba the locals at the

Syrtaki and should stick to the old slow-slow-quick-quick or to bopping away in his usual time-tested fashion to the rhythm of this season's foot-tapper.

Not that there'll be much joy to be got from this season's foot-tapper. Usually you will have recognised and identified that particular tune within an hour of arrival at your resort, and for the first day you may even quite like it. Savour the first day then, because you are unlikely to like it ever again. Nor, for the rest of your holiday, will you ever be able to get it out of your head. Even for the most Untypical Tourist there is no escape. Every second song on the radio, at the disco, at the nightclub will be *that* song. The strains coming through your bedroom window as you try to sleep, or going round in your head preventing you from sleeping, will always be *that* song.

It will linger on in your mind long after that glorious summer in Ouzo-la-mer, always liable to be set off by some chance remark, reminding you yet again of that particular holiday of a lifetime.

In his search for romance 'by night', the Typical Tourist can find himself in some pretty low locales – the sort of place you feel improperly dressed if you're not carrying a switchblade and where it's assumed, if you're on your own, that you must be looking for something.

This is precisely the appeal of those after-hours bars. They're essentially for people in a marauding mood, somewhere for the Typical Tourist to insult the locals with his money (they're only too glad to be insulted), play Bogart, talk to the person on the neighbouring bar stool through the barman. ('Buy the lady champagne.') She, however, will probably address him directly when she proposes: 'Tu viens chez moi, chéri?'

It's these sort of dubious adventures which often provide the Typical Tourist with the best holiday memories, or, sometimes, which provide the best memories of that time when his or her spouse went off on holiday. For we should not forget the ones who stay behind. As the French know the *'vrais couples d'août'* are the ones who stay in Paris.

The Spaniards call it the Rodriguez phenomenon. (For some reason, an awful lot of Spanish men, left behind in Madrid for the summer while the wives take the children off to the coast, start calling themselves Rodriguez – the Spanish equivalent of Smith or Jones. *Curioso, no?*)

But it's not just a few *pères de famille* who enjoy the Rodriguez season. The children do too: it's said that August is when many continental toyshops do their best business – with guilty fathers buying little somethings for their offspring to quieten their consciences.

But in the end, perhaps, the real reason why those amorous entanglements on holiday are so fondly remembered is that they have to be so promptly disentangled. Thus you don't have to spend a lot of time worrying how you're going to end the affair. And both parties can happily pack their bags and go their separate ways, while at the same time, of course, vowing everlasting love.

14
Bathing

'Man can't live by bread alone. You need beaches'
Voiceover to the film *Muscle Beach*

ALONG WITH sightseeing, shopping, romance, and guzzling, bathing must rank as one of the most popular of holiday activities. There's a compulsive urge in most Typical Tourists, wherever they are, to head for the water's edge, be it lake, river or sea.

This may, however, be a bit less true than it was. Since a tan ceased to be the exclusive privilege of the rich and leisured classes, it's not just the occasional Untypical Tourist who prefers to remain pale and interesting. Nevertheless, for vast numbers of holidaymakers, a tan will be the most precious possession they bring back with them from abroad.

They will have worked for it. When the Typical Tourist's colleagues at the office remark on how brown he looks, he will probably try to look surprised, seeking to convey that any tanning was incidental, something picked up casually, while going about his normal holiday business. 'Have I really got a tan,' he will exclaim, 'I hadn't realised, but we did have one or two nice days.'

There'll be no hint of how he anxiously scanned the horizon for possible clouds every morning, and then spent every last minute of his daytime hours prostrate amid the mingled scents of suntain oil and frying flesh, moving only when it was time to turn over and do the other side or apply one of his many lotions.

The sheer professionalism with which many Typical Tourists go about this basting process is almost beyond belief. Alarm-clock timing to indicate when to turn over or grease up; bits of plastic or Bako foil to put on those places they forgot to anoint (like nose); special mirrors on rods to inspect their backs; the latest information on ECT (Estimated Cloud Time); and, of course, a variety of lotions – everything from local concoctions, like a mixture of olive oil and vinegar, to coconut butter or Bergamot oil, and the latest products of tanning research and technology (all with Factor numbers and doubtful claims to intensify the UVA tanning rays, cut out the UVB non-tanning rays, maximise vitamin D intake, or reduce the danger of skin cancer).

None of this will be revealed to the Typical Tourist's office colleagues as he casually confesses that he did spend a certain amount of time lounging around in the sun. There'll be no admitting the amount of work put in to get in shape for the beach and then the hours of sheer boredom just lying there alongside the other bodies carpeting the shore; or how he had to sleep standing up; or the agonies endured when those third-degree burns came into contact with the bed sheets; or the amount of calamine lotion put on after beach hours; or his self-pitying reflections about how right those Victorian Brits were never to expose themselves to the fierce sun of abroad, unless they were wearing their topees and spine pads to protect them from its harmful rays.

The one thing that can be said for sunbathing, though, is that it's not an activity that disturbs anyone else – except possibly the local moralists who dislike the idea of people getting those all-over tans that are now becoming so popular. (Remember how revolutionary it seemed when the bikini first appeared on the scene, not so many years ago.)

Plenty of other beach activities are a good deal more disturbing – particularly on the big 'action' beaches (the Bondis, Copacabanas, Waikikis, etc.) where everyone will be constantly on the go. Thus the Untypical Tourist tends to stick to the Riviera type of *'bronze-cul'* beach like Tahiti Plage where the beautiful people just go to see and be seen, and lie there in rows without bothering each other too much. (Not that these beaches are exclusive to the beautiful people of course – you also see plenty of women *d'un certain âge* going defiantly topless, and looking to the sun to cover their varicose veins.)

Action beaches tend to be popular with families and large groups who arrive like a band of migrating settlers, laden with equipment and playthings to keep themselves occupied – card tables, folding chairs, charcoal grills and barbecue sets, air-mattresses, raffia beach mats, hammocks, tents, windbreaks, cooking pots and utensils, transistor radios, cassette players, portable televisions, buckets, spades, bats, balls, nets, cool-boxes, abundant food supply and so on.

As much as anything else, the purpose of all this equipment is to stake out and occupy an area of territory which other families will invade at their peril. It's interesting on any beach to watch the hostile stares given by the recumbent incumbents to any approaching new arrivals looking for a place to park themselves.

These extended family beach groups are very busy organisations, with everyone constantly on the move. It'll take them half an hour to decide which way the wind's coming, then an hour to blow up the mattresses, to erect the umbrella, the windbreak, and the tent, and to set up the rest of the camp. It'll then take a while to get dressed, or rather undressed (with everyone taking turns to change under the sun-tents and sundresses), to put on their beach hats and to smear each other with oil. After that, there'll be no let up, as they set about their allotted tasks – organising one another, playing with the children, stopping children's tears, getting the grill going, finding out what everyone wants to eat, preparing food, feeding one another, settling disputes about which radio programme or cassette to listen to, playing games, and so on.

In fact, there won't be much peace to be found anywhere on an action beach. As well as these tribal groups, there'll always be plenty of people doing exercises, or jogging, or trampolining, or flying kites, or playing with rackets and balls, or kicking sand into one another's faces, or trying to slice the top of your head off with a frisbee, or building sandcastles, or making human pyramids.

And then there are all the dogs, children, thieves, hustlers and ice-cream sellers all making a nuisance of themselves.

No beach, even if it is 3-star EEC-approved, is without its hazards. In the water you can be attacked by sea-urchins, sharks, jellyfish or, more likely, by surfers, wind-surfers, parachuters, water-skiers, pedalo-drivers, scuba-divers or harpoon-snorklers or, more likely still, by the oil and general pollution. (It can only be a matter of time, surely, before the sea becomes semi-solid.)

On the beach itself there is danger lurking at every turn. Take, for instance, those innocent-looking and inviting lollipop-striped beach chairs; in fact, as the Untypical Tourist knows only too well, their sagging canvas and rickety frames are just waiting to give out on you, trapping your finger or causing severe injury to some other part of your anatomy.

Sand, too, is tricky stuff. In theory it's fun, and the Typical Tourist looks forward to wiggling his toes in it, but it's also very messy (one reason why many beautiful people or professional tanners prefer to do their thing at a marina, pool, bunch of rocks, bathing establishment, or from their yacht). Sand gets everywhere – in your shoes, in your pockets, in your ears, in your hair, in between your toes, into your sandwiches, in your Thermos flask, and sticks particularly readily to any part of your body that's been carefully anointed with oil.

At times it will burn the bottom of your feet off, or it will turn out not really to be sand but little stones instead, which will cut your feet to ribbons. It will also, frequently, be dirty. Although beaches are supposed to be golden, most are any other colour but golden. You realise why when you look at the underside of your feet on getting back to your room. You discover that although the approach road to the beach may not have been tarred, the beach certainly was. You suddenly realise what all those people were doing scraping their feet on those kerosene-soaked brushes outside your hotel.

Ironically, beaches were probably a lot safer in the days when they were considered potentially unsafe – when they were 'prescribed' by doctors, something to be taken in moderation and to which you exposed yourself practically fully clothed, and from the seclusion of a bathing hut on wheels. Today, when we've been conditioned to equate beaches with good health, to let it all hang out, to do what comes naturally, we get nothing but trouble. Far from being health-giving, they're probably a major health risk. Georve V knew what he was talking about when he said: 'Bugger Bognor'.

As a result many Untypical Tourists have given up beaches altogether, or, if not, at least restrict their beach-going to early or late in the day – the times when the picture-postcard photographers appear, when the tide is out and there's no-one else around.

15
Travel Advice

'Streets full of water. Advise'
Robert Benchley, cabling home from Venice

IN ORDER to keep their travel troubles to a minimum, many Typical Tourists turn to one of those many handbooks for travellers which seem to be written especially for life's pessimists – the sort of people who set off with about fifteen rolls of toilet paper in their luggage.

Invariably, these books' main prescription for avoiding abroad's evils and ensuring a trouble-free holiday is to devote a lot of time to making lists. These travel advisers (many of them American) are among the world's greatest list-makers. They'll encourage the Typical Tourist to view his holiday as a sort of expedition and to start making his lists several months before departure – lists of what to take, what to buy, what to see, what to do, what to say, what to pay.

The Untypical Tourist knows better than to take these books too seriously. Clearly they are written by highly organised sensible people, but their advice can at times seem a bit superfluous. Do we really need to be told to take comfortable shoes (who's for uncomfortable shoes?); or to tell the police and your embassy if you lose your passport (who else?); or to lock up your home properly before you go (should we leave the front door open?).

And you can be sure there will always be one major contradiction in their advice: they'll tell you to travel light, and then give you an enormous list of things to take with you.

Very often their advice can seem a bit far-fetched – like telling you to take a set of winter clothes and a set of summer clothes, so that when you've got to Ouzo and found out what the weather's like, you can mail one set home. Some also suggest you mail your dirty linen home – though they don't say what to do when you run out.

Nor, as the Untypical Tourist knows only too well, are their recommendations always entirely disinterested. Many of the genial hosts mentioned in their books will have provided the author with a free meal, or a free bed for the night, which means they won't want to say anything too unkind about these establishments.

The Untypical Tourist is also wary of the authors' claims to fluency in many tongues; these claims are usually belied by the fact that most of the foreign words in their books will be spelt wrong.

On occasion, of course, the author won't even have been to some of the places mentioned. This, however, need not matter too much. Defoe's *Madagascar*, for instance, is one of the best descriptions of an island on which the author never set foot.

And whether the author has actually been there or not, he should at least be able to give you valuable advance warning about some of the nasties that lie ahead. Thus you can make sure not to be in Ouzo for the Wailing Festival, or for Hunt-the-Tourist week, or during the International Pickpocket Association's annual conference.

At all events these books will almost certainly be more help to you than the local guidebooks, characterised by their rather offbeat English, inviting you to 'enjoy memories of gay revels, in snug wine taverns, just like your good old student days, in our traditional town, in this country blessed from the Nature'.

Even less helpful will be those giveaway booklets or magazines left in hotel lobbies or in your bedroom, with titles like 'In Town' or 'What's On'. A better name would be 'What to Avoid', since they're usually no more than a list of all the major local rip-offs – 'American' bars, nightspots with hostesses, 'private' clubs, 'free' tours of factories or workshops (selling diamonds, glass, dolls, furs, leather, etc.), 'exclusive' 15%-off discount houses, certificate-issuing 'antique' shops, rejuvenation treatments, massage and other 'services'.

As we said earlier, however, for some Typical Tourists, getting ripped off is what a holiday is all about. For them, being sensible would take all the fun out of it. Some travellers prefer to be incompetent travellers, regardless of all the pain and suffering that may entail. If you want to be sure which type you are, here's a checklist to help you decide:

The Competent Traveller	*The Incompetent Traveller*
speaks the local language	wishes he'd remembered to bring his phrasebook along
registers with the British Embassy on arrival	makes himself known to the British Embassy when he runs out of money
gives his children a whistle	is only too happy when his children get lost
never runs out of film	spends a lot of time asking friends if they have a spare roll
travels with several copies of Form E 111	has never heard of Form E 111

has all the jabs anyone is prepared to give him	has always wondered about that little orange booklet that some people carry around inside their passports
knows his blood group	believes in looking on the bright side
takes with him a very complete first-aid kit	rubs toothpaste in his wounds and believes in purifying the water by putting alcohol in it
has a lot of insurance	trusts to luck
knows the emergency number of whatever country he's in	believes in shouting for help
checks the earthquake fault lines before he goes	believes that when you gotta go, you gotta go
knows by heart the number, date and place of issue of his passport	can never remember these details, which is unfortunate since his passport is often buried at the bottom of his *other* bag
has an up-to-date visa	didn't know you needed one
carries a copy of his birth certificate	doesn't even have a copy of his birth certificate at home
has a pen handy to fill in forms	clambers over everyone to rifle through his suitcase, and then borrows one
has a picture of the local dictator in his wallet, in case of any conflicts with local officials	has no hesitation in denouncing any bothersome officials as Fascist pigs
asks troublesome officials their name	asks troublesome officials who the Hell they think they are
argues about the cab fare beforehand	argues afterwards

always knows the day's exchange rate	can never remember the name of the local currency
compares the rates at several banks before changing money, and only does so on days when it's favourable	always changes at the hotel (which charges the most outrageous commission), or changes on the black market (and gets diddled, or arrested)
travels with a letter of credit from his bank 'just in case'	doesn't have a bank that would write him a letter of credit, even if he knew what one was
makes a note of the numbers of his travellers cheques	takes cash as he never remembers to order travellers cheques in time
always has small denominations of local currency on him	often finds himself leaning out of the window, as the train pulls out of the station, desperately negotiating to buy a bottle of mineral water, when all he has on him is a 100,000 note, and the vendor says he hasn't any change
knows a little place where they knock off 10%	buys in the hotel souvenir shop
has an overseas telephone credit card	can never get the hang of the local *jeton* system, so pays five times over the odds to phone from his hotel and keeps on getting interrupted by the operator saying 'Have you finished?'
makes a note of his air-ticket number	didn't know his air-ticket had a number
reconfirms his reservation within seventy-two hours of flying	wonders why he's always the one to get bumped
knows his flight number	has difficulty enough remembering his destination
is familiar with the details of the 1929 Warsaw convention	never took much interest in central European history

arrives at the airport two hours before take-off	squeaks on to the plane about a minute before they close the flight
on being bumped asks the airline for a written statement setting out its policy on denied boarding compensation and its boarding priorities	wonders why it always happens to him, and why the law is always on the airline's side
has a special mark on his suitcase to help him identify it quickly (as well as having it clearly labelled outside and in)	frequently walks off with the wrong suitcase, or watches it go round on the baggage hall conveyor belt five times before identifying it
carries pocket scales to check that his luggage is not overweight	hopes for the best
has a list of everything he has with him, in case his luggage gets lost	would use his imagination if this happened
notes the number of his porter's badge	never could tell one foreigner from another
makes lists for the customs	doesn't make lists for himself, let alone for the customs
has sales receipts for his camera and watch (however many years ago he bought them)	has never kept a sales receipt in his life, and doesn't intend to start now
gets a room with a view on the quiet side of the hotel	gets a room over the kitchen, or the disco, or next to the lift-shaft
has a nylon clothes line to hang out his washing over the bath, and slips the chambermaid a few bob so she won't tell	causes an international incident by hanging his washing out of the hotel window to dry
places the mattresses crossways, when pushing two single beds together	crashes to the floor with his loved one, when the beds fly apart in the middle of the night

pays his hotel bill the night before	queues for three-quarters of an hour to pay it in the morning
checks the bill	assumes the bill is wrong, but pays up anyway
when in dispute asks to see the man's superior	believes they're all as bad as one another
makes life difficult for the natives	let's the natives make life difficult for him
believes 'you never know' and takes with him a vast assortment of 'just-in-case' supplies – everything from salt tablets to spare shoe laces.	has none of these things. Does not even have a dictionary so he can ask for them. Believes in travelling light, and improvising, and making friends with a competent tourist, so he can borrow in case of need

16
Transport

'The great and recurrent question about Abroad is, is it worth the trouble of getting there?'
Rose Macaulay, *Personal Pleasures*

PROBABLY THE worst thing about abroad is the awful business of getting around – trains and boats and planes and all that. Not so, that it's better to travel than to arrive. *Getting* there is almost always a damn sight worse than *being* there.

As with most aspects of travel, there's the illusion and there's the reality. Motorists see themselves hitting the Continent like rally drivers, with the top down, the sun on their faces, the wind in their hair, and nothing but the open road between them and the Med. Notions about boats and trains also date from a bygone age. People imagine themselves sailing P and O in its imperial heyday, lascars scrubbing away at their feet, or in one of those transcontinental wood-panelled wagons-lits, bound for romance and adventure amid the mists of Middle Europe. The supposed glamour of flying also dates from the days before everyone was doing it.

But travel is not what it was, or rather, is not what we like to think it was. Someone once described travelling with children as being like travelling third class in Bulgaria. Well, these days, just about *all* travel feels like travelling third class in Bulgaria. And that's at the start of your journey – things tend to get worse as you go on.

Planes

'If God had meant us to travel tourist class he would have made us narrower' Martha Zimmerman, *American air stewardess*

Perhaps the greatest pleasure to be derived from air travel these days is in finding ways to try to beat the system. The Untypical Tourist knows you won't succeed – but it's fun trying. This game starts well before you climb aboard, as you comb the small ads, and do the the rounds of the bucket shops, comparing the merits and the catches of Apex, Superapex, Underapex, Overapex, frills, no frills, extra frills, all frills, walk-on, walk-off, excursion, special excursion, excursion special, fly-drive, drive-fly, etc.

One thing is sure. Even if you've got the sort of mind that can get to grips with the Warsaw Convention, you'll never be able to figure out the system. This is largely because the airlines and operators keep changing the rules. You finally get the hang of Catch 22 ('You can have Nopex, provided you come back on the second Wednesday of the month with no baggage to check in and provided there are spare seats in Superapex'); then you suddenly find it has turned into Catch 23 (now it's provided there are *no* spare seats in Superapex).

There was a time, supposedly, a sort of Golden Age of Air Travel, before this type of sordid wrangling became one of the main features of flying. In those days, so it is believed, flying was comfortable and quick. There was no bumping or stacking. Times of arrival were times of arrival – not *estimated* times of arrival. Stewardesses were glamour girls, not just waitresses in the sky. Airports were built on a human scale – they were not huge anonymous multi-terminal miniature cities set in a sort of international limbo.

To judge by accounts of the Golden Days of Air Travel, choosing your seat *used* to be a matter of sheer wish-fulfilment. Stewardesses would take a pride and a pleasure, particularly if you were travelling on your own, in matching you up with someone compatible, and starting off many of those legendary aeroplane romances. Nowadays they seem to get their kicks from deliberately *not* doing so.

On the whole, therefore, it's probably best to simply state a preference for smoking or non-smoking, aisle or window (does anyone ever ask for the middle seat?), and let the check-in desk do their worst. But the know-it-all, Typical Tourist will often make the most of this golden moment of choice to try to get a seat with more leg-room by the emergency exit, or to get put next to a seat that's likely to remain empty, or one of those seats at the rear where they say you have the best chance of survival. The Untypical Tourist knows that, unless he can claim health reasons, it's usually too late to get the seats with leg-room, and any attempts to get put next to empty seats usually mean that the checker will take great pleasure in putting you next to someone very large, or hysterical, or with an extraordinary amount of hand-luggage.

Many Typical Tourists make the mistake of going for the front seat. This inevitably means ending up next to a family with children. If the stewardess takes a dislike to you, this is one of the places she'll try to put you, or next to the loo, or next to the movie screen.

Finally, boarding card clamped between your teeth, you're off to passport control and then to security, to get frisked and pass through the x-ray screen. Compared with airline staff, who tend to think rather too highly of themselves, security people are usually very pleasant and don't normally cause the tourists any trouble – apart from occasionally asking them to take some metal out of their pocket and to go past the magnetometer a second time. It may be that they're just happy to have a job; thanks to the hijackers, airport security has become very much a growth industry.

You now find yourself in the departure lounge, that antechamber of the skies, for what will probably be a long wait. It may be the departure lounge which gives some people their notions about the glamour of air-travel. Those display cases of 'luxury' goods and the duty-free shop with its super-length cigarettes and jumbo-size bottles of booze make you feel like someone with money to spend. And there's also the sense of being one up on the people at home, though it's hard to see how people can get so excited about the prospect of such meagre financial advantage – if indeed there is any: some airport shops even charge VAT on goods bought, and many conveniently blur the distinction between duty-free and tax-free; and some are a lot less cheap than others (there are even prices which vary between Gatwick and Heathrow.)

Gradually your flight will creep up the departure board and eventually the light will start flashing, and it will be called – invariably after a number of announcements regretting to inform you that, for technical reasons, or reasons outside anyone's control, your flight has been delayed. (This is most likely to happen at Christmas and Easter, the traditional times for disruption at airports, and when the air-traffic controllers like to get themselves in the news, and endear themselves to the travelling public.)

On boarding, you'll get your free nod, word or smile of welcome from the stewardess (or perhaps steward – there are more and more of them about) and discover where you're sitting: if you're a 'top person' towards the front in First class, Executive class, Club class, Business class, Clipper class or whatever it's called. And if you're not such a top person in Tourist class, Peasant class, Lucky-to-be-on-board class or Standby. Planes do tend to be rather class-conscious places.

The Untypical Tourist knows, however, that where you sit is rather less important than who you are sitting next to (ideally, of course, no one – if the plane is half full). If you're unlucky, you may find yourself next to a drunk; an hysteric; a compulsive talker; a clutcher; a messy-eater; someone who gets airsick; an airplane bore who's flown 'em all and keeps on reminiscing about the days of Dakotas; someone with eight items of hand-baggage; someone who insists that his forearm and elbow occupy the whole of the seatrest; someone with a window-seat who needs to go to the loo every five minutes or keeps climbing on top of you to get something out of the pocket of his jacket in the overhead rack; someone who produces an eye-shade and spills over into your territory as he curls up with his smelly socks; a gum-chewer with breathing problems who has to clean out his nasal passages and sinuses with a spray before take-off; or two would-be members of the Mile High Club. Or you may be a non-smoker who finds he's across the aisle from, or directly in front of, a row of heavy smokers with all the smoke blowing in your direction. Or you may find yourself behind someone who keeps on bouncing up and down in his seat and likes to recline it at mealtimes so that his or her dandruff or hair lacquer flicks off into your blancmange. Or you may be in front of someone who specialises in driving his knee into the back of the seat in front. Or there may be lots of children in the vicinity (who, surprisingly enough, will often find their unruly behaviour rewarded with a visit to the cockpit).

The cabin staff, however, will try to keep you distracted from these irritations.

There'll be those amusing announcements with built-in deliberate mistakes, the oxygen mask demonstration, a few words from the captain, the flight plan to pass round, a form or two to fill in, an invitation to crane your neck to look at Düsseldorf or Mont Blanc as we fly past (it's invariably on the other side of the plane), the hot towels or damp cleansing paper, music, the movie and whatever else passes for in-flight entertainment.

Then there are always a number of free toys to play with. The longer the flight, the more there are. There's the in-flight magazine, the free flight bag, the little cushion, postcards, eyemask, slipper socks, shoe-horn, toothbrush and paste, aftershave and so on.

The more you pay, the more things you get to play with, and the better you're treated. First-class passengers are known by name, get bigger smiles from the stewardesses, more space, free cigarettes and, above all, a sense of superiority. Charter passengers, by comparison, find themselves squashed together on wonky seats on geriatric, grime-streaked jets, with just a meal and a flight mag to keep them amused, and a less attractive stewardess to complain to.

The main way the airline will try to keep the Typical Tourist amused and occupied during the flight will be by feeding him – despite the fact that the doctors say you shouldn't eat during a flight, and should just drink water (to offset the dehydration of the pressurised cabin). Most passengers, however, would get very upset if they weren't fed, or provided with the means to get quietly sloshed. (This is often what people mean when they say they like flying – what they're really saying is they like drinking.)

Feeding time is also when you come into closest contact with the stewardess. They're a funny breed – not, of course, what they were in the Golden Days of Air Travel, but very definitely with ideas above their station.

They tend to see the passengers as oversized children, to be strapped into their chairs, to be fed, to be told off, ignored, refused second helpings, or sometimes given even stiffer punishment by being bumped with the trolley. The aim is to subdue you, drug you, quieten you down, and send you to sleep, so that you don't disturb their daydreams about getting into the sack with the first officer and how much they can make stripping the plane after the flight.

Really it would be infinitely preferable to have some friendly old biddy who likes looking after people, or even one of those highly competent *babushkas* who seem to run Russian railways, and who bring you glasses of tea from time to time, rather than some bathing beauty who believes you have an ulterior motive in asking for a second bread roll. Most stewardesses seem to believe that their male clients are really not after 'coffee' or 'tea', but 'me'.

Thus it's always something of a challenge to obtain some extra service from the stewardess. Your success here will be largely determined by how much you've paid. Are you in front of, or behind, the magic dividing curtain? If you're back in Prole class, it's liable to be an uphill job persuading the stewardess that you're a person of some importance, and deserve special attention.

Another thing that keeps a lot of people busy is worrying: about the cracks in the wing; about those roars and clunks on take-off and landing. We all know there are supposed to be roars and clunks, but are they the *right* roars and clunks? Does the airport have ground radar or not? Failsafe is not a word that most of us place much credence in.

Statistics may show that our chances of copping it are only three in a million, but most of us know perfectly well that they're far greater than that. Most of us realise that our chances of crashing, or being hi-jacked, are about one in three. And we all know, deep down, whatever anyone else may say about road accidents or natural causes, that if we're going to die, the chances are it'll be in an aircrash.

We all know what it'll be like. We'll be grasping helplessly for those dangling oxygen masks, and fumbling unsuccessfully with our life-jackets and trying to work out how to open the emergency door, and cursing ourselves for not having paid more attention when the stewardess gave her demonstration, and for not having read the emergency instructions in the seat-pocket in front of us.

Meanwhile the plane will spiral into an even steeper nosedive. The pilot will be fighting a losing battle as he wrestles with his joystick. (Or whatever they have these days. Come to think of it, do they still have real human pilots in there, or are those announcements recorded?) At all events, this is the sort of scenario we conjure up every time we hear that announcement beginning: 'This is your captain speaking'.

Therefore it's usually quite a relief when he brings us down safely. We may not burst into applause, like they often do on charters, but we certainly feel that way. The relief will be momentary, however. Having diced with death and survived, we're soon ready to ignore the warning that 'for our own safety and comfort' (comfort?) we should 'remain seated with our seatbelts fastened until the aircraft has come to a complete stop' and prepare to do battle again to get out of the aircraft, and through yet another airport.

Trains

'What earthly enjoyment was there in travelling – being jolted about in stuffy trains . . .?' Jerome K. Jerome, *Diary of a Pilgrimage*

In their day, trains were probably the equivalent of today's planes, the last word in high-speed luxury travel, with smartly turned-out attendants and stewards offering service in the Grand Manner. The Golden Arrow, the Orient Express and the Blue Train were the equivalents of Concorde and the latest Boeing super-jumbo. Those huge nineteenth-century metropolitan railway stations were the equivalent of today's airports, with their restaurants, bars, barbershops, shoe-shine parlours, and displays of luxury goods. And as at airports, there would also be a big hotel or two just outside the terminus. Today, however, the average Railway Hotel is usually somewhat less ritzy than its Aerogolf equivalent, and the same goes for trains.

It's true that trains have tried to move with the times. We've gone from chuff-chuff to diesel, and from diesel to various kinds of superpowered *trains à grande vitesse*. But somehow most trains and railway stations still tend to be coated with the grime of the Industrial Age rather than the gloss of the Space Age.

The attraction of travelling by train is that you're left more to your own devices, not just strapped into your seat, fed, and ordered around (except for that notice telling you not to lean out of the window in four languages). There's also more to see out of the window. And you're less worried about the prospect of imminent death than on planes. You can move about more, leave your compartment for the no-man's-land of the corridor, walk along the train, even get off to stretch your legs on the platform at longer stops. (Sometimes, of course, you'll be forced to do so – when the trains splits up, and you find that your carriage is not going where *you're* going.)

Trains are also, somehow, a more suitable venue than planes for assignations, romantic or otherwise – there's an air of conspiracy about trains. You certainly get more chance to choose the company you keep. Before boarding you can inspect each coach and compartment as you work your way down the train, deciding either to settle for one that already seems reasonably congenially occupied, or to pick an empty one and run the risk of being invaded by people you may not like.

The trick, of course, if you're not feeling sociable, is to try to deter any would-be travelling companions. The usual Untypical Tourist technique is to pull down the blinds and spread yourself around – luggage, coat, papers all over the place, making it look as if your six companions have just nipped out for a quick one. You then stare frostily at anyone who peeks inside, daring them to ask 'Is this seat taken?', and trying to convey that you'd be rather objectionable company.

You can also spread out your provisions (trains tend to attract picnickers, who usually make for the window-seat with the table flap). A lot of people will be put off by the prospect of sitting next to someone who looks as if he'll spend the whole journey munching away at his tomatoes. You can also take your shoes off, and put your feet on the seat opposite, and take off various other items of clothing (the Japanese are the great specialists at undressing in trains). The prospect of having to suffer the pong of someone's feet, or armpits, is probably an even greater deterrent than the prospect of having to suffer the pong of their Gorgonzola, or of getting wine spilt all over them.

You won't be bothered on trains by stewards or stewardesses, but you will have the odd brush with a ticket-collector and, when you cross borders, with police and customs officials. There will also be those itinerant peddlers with their sandwich carts or 'mini-bars' offering you *demi-baguettes* wrapped in greaseproof paper and bottles of Pschitt or Perrier at outrageous prices, and charging you double if you don't have the right currency.

If you want to be even more outraged, you can go along to the restaurant or buffet car. Another intinerant, sometimes equipped with a little bell, will pass along the train at intervals, announcing that lunch or dinner is served. You tend to obey the steward's summons more because eating is a way of passing the time than because you really want to. This is just as well. Not many railway systems plumb the same culinary depths as British Rail, but they all work at it. And the service, these days, is rarely in the Grand Manner. No velvet curtains, damask tablecloths and silver salvers. The waiters may still have epaulettes on their tunics, but they'll certainly have soup stains on them as well. You probably will, too, by the time you've finished: trains traditionally like to start you off with soup – perhaps for the pleasure of seeing how you cope, trying to synchronise each mouthful with the roll and bump of the train.

If dining on trains is not what it was, nor is sleeping. Those individual or duplex varnished teak sleeping compartments of old have given way to multi-occupancy units, most notably the couchette. The result is that you can spend as much time rearranging the compartment as you do lying down. It usually takes a good while to discover how to unfold the bunks and make them up with what passes for bed linen. You then have to work out where to put the luggage, now that you've lost half of your storage space.

After that there'll be the long debates about who sleeps on top and who sleeps below, before everyone starts on their pre-bed rituals. (Some people go through exactly the same routine as they would at home – even changing into their pyjamas.) When you do eventually get the lights off, there'll be very little sleeping done. You spend most of your time wondering whose feet smell so bad, and who's doing the snoring. The temperature will never be right – it'll be too hot or too cold, and nothing you can do to any of the levers in the compartment will make the slightest difference to this. And trains do, of course, make an infernal noise. You'll also be disturbed at regular intervals by people opening the door of your compartment, looking inside, switching on the lights, and then slamming the door shut again. All a far cry from travelling on the old Orient Express where an eagle-eyed attendant sat at the end of each carpeted corridor ensuring that his clients suffered no night-time intrusions, and was always ready to use his Balkan wits – at a price, of course – to meet any additional requirements they might have. Still, you should perhaps be glad if the worst that happens to you is a sleepless night: we've all heard about those thieves who specialise in squirting some noxious gas into a sleeping compartment and ripping off both Typical and Untypical Tourists while they're unconscious.

Driving

'For many years the French have been playing something called auto soccer. The sport, which originated at the Place de la République and spread all the way over to the Porte de St. Cloud, requires the participants to hit a pedestrian and then try to push him into the other fellow's goal.'
Art Buchwald, *Down the Seine and up the Potomac*

Driving is perhaps the mode of transport where you get most to grips with the enemy – particularly if you take the byways rather than the highways in order to 'see the country'. Even those Brits (probably the majority), who pace the deck impatiently throughout the Channel crossing, and intend to bomb straight on down to Ouzo, usually find they make only halting progress when they get ashore. Those Euro-roads always turn out to have more caravanners and fume-belching artics gumming them up than you would ever have thought possible.

A variety of mishaps will befall you en route but your biggest worry is likely to be the vagaries of foreign drivers. (Whichever country you're in at the time, of course, will have the world's worst.) There are those Germans who scream down the fast lane of the *Autobahn* in their big Mercedes, lights flashing angrily at anyone in their path; the Belgians, who used to get their driving licences out of cornflake packets, and specialise in doing the totally unexpected; the Dutch with their caravans, who crawl along from picnic stop to picnic stop trying to achieve zero petrol consumption; the Scandinavians in their big station wagons, who believe you can drive from one end of Europe to another in a day; the Spaniards, with their jack-knifing trucks and their habit of driving in the middle of the road; the French, bouncing around in their elastically-sprung battle-scarred cars, masters of urban driving, switching lanes fearlessly and respecting no rule save that of *priorité à droite* (even when, according to the new law, it's really *priorité à gauche*); the Luxemburgers, with their even more obsessive *priorité à droite* – only, in fact, ever looking to the right; the Italians, the world's greatest horn-honkers, who also excel at in-town driving and have a genius for near misses; the Greeks, who spend as much time arguing and conveying non-verbal messages to one another as they do driving; the Swiss, with their metallic silver-grey cars, never more than eighteen months old, all tinted windows and blinds and curtains, with ski-racks on top and snow-tyres and chains in the boot; ditto the Austrians, except that their cars are older, don't have tinted windows or blinds and their driving is much much worse; and the various nationalities of migrant workers limping along as fast as they can go, their tenth-hand used cars packed with people or consumer durables or both, and all their personal belongings tied on the roof with string (which is also used to hold bits of the car together).

These days British cars, or frequently minibuses, seem to bear most resemblance to those of the migrant workers. For Brits also drive some of the older vehicles on the road, often decorated with dangling dollies and the odd slogan. They also specialise in racking all their gear on the roof, equipped as for a major expedition. They, too, travel, in numbers and usually have a couple of children stowed away somewhere.

In other respects, however, Brits are not so easily outdone by the Continentals, and even the mildest mannered have learnt to trade insult for insult, blow for blow with the best of them. Today's Briton abroad is no slouch in pulling alongside and rolling down his window for an exchange of views (one advantage of right-hand drive), has no hesitation in making those views clear with gestures if necessary, and even seems to be coming round to the continental view that it's possible to clear a traffic jam by persistent use of your hooter.

For Brits there's also the added challenge of having to drive on the wrong side of the road; and learning the hard way about continental rules for entering roundabouts; or about *priorité à droite* (when some peasant on a tractor confidently crosses your path from a dirt road to your right forcing you to screech to a halt on the main road.) These sort of difficulties often lead to friction *within* the car, as well as with other drivers. There will be frequent occasions when you will call into question your navigator's map-reading ability and, on occasion, his or her sanity – for instance after a bad piece of overtaking advice ('Yes. Now. OK. Go. No. Sorry. Back. B-a-c-k!').

Despite these frustrations, however, there is a certain comradeliness on the open road. People with the same type of car, and other Britons abroad, will flash their lights at you in recognition. (This is not to be confused with foreigners flashing their lights at you in exasperation – because you haven't black-taped your headlamps, or adjusted your beam for driving on the right, or because your white low beams are too bright for them.)

There'll be no camaraderie in the towns, however, where you'll be at daggers drawn with other drivers. As the foreigner you're bound to be in the wrong, and therefore a legitimate target for abuse. But in the end, they'll just say 'damned Brits', shrug their shoulders and go on their way. This is one of the pleasures of driving in foreign towns. You can misbehave with impunity. With your foreign plates, you can usually park on double, triple or quadruple yellow lines, without too much risk of being towed away, or having your licence plates removed, or your wheel clamped. Actually, this is not quite so true as it was. (Beware, for instance, of Italian green zones.) But, in general, traffic wardens seem to feel you'd be a waste of a ticket, as they'd never get their money. It's not just diplomats who don't pay their parking fines. Some countries have come to accept that a parking ticket for a foreigner is just another piece of waste paper for the glove compartment: in Paris and Copenhagen, for instance, they now leave little notes on your windscreen saying something like 'You're really not supposed to park here, but as you're a foreigner we'll let you off. Have a nice time in our city.' Speeding fines are less easy to get out of, as a lot of police now fine you on the spot, often being harsher to foreigners than to the locals (and they want *cash* – no cheques or credit cards).

Nor will you be able to avoid a certain amount of physical damage – getting bumped and scraped, having your tyres slashed, your aerial snapped, your radio nicked (almost certain to happen if you're in Italy) and your windshield wipers stolen (an East European speciality). And if you break down in open country in the East, never leave your car unattended, or it won't just be your windshield wipers that will go; the natives can cannibalise a temporarily abandoned car in about twenty minutes flat.

Boats

'Getting there is half the fun' Advertisement for Cunard Steamship Line

There are two basic kinds of boat travel – where you take the boat somewhere, or where the boat takes you somewhere.

The first category covers everything from messing around in small craft (sculls, catamarans, rowing-boats, dinghies, motor-boats, cruisers, yachts) right up to large rented barges, or the kind of luxury yacht where you pay other people to crew and sail them about for you. The main aim is always to have fun messing around in a boat, rather than to get from A to B. How much fun you have depends on the role allotted to you – captain, crew, mate, cook, galley-slave. Inevitably, it's the skipper, wearing his sailor hat, giving the orders, and showing off his nautical know-how, who has the most fun. His pre-eminence, of course, usually owes less to his sailing skill than to the fact that he's the owner. The others have less fun – more or less in proportion to where they rank in the hierarchy. If you don't like hierarchies you won't have very much fun at all. Boats, especially small ones, are very hierarchical places.

In the second category – where the boat takes you somewhere – the passengers are not actually involved in sailing the boat around, and the main purpose is often to get from A to B, i.e. crossing the Channel on ferry, hovercraft or hydrofoil or, less likely these days, the ocean on liner or cargo boat.

This category also includes the cruise ship, where instead of being busy sailing you spend your time eating, drinking and socialising with your fellow passengers; getting sick; taking a turn round the deck; staring out to sea; playing deck quoits and shuffleboard; and studying yet again the chart showing the ship's position, before placing your bet on the ship's daily mileage.

The people who have the most fun on cruises, and on whom most interest is focused, seem to be the people who have a real job to do – the captain and his various officers. One of the passengers' main aims is to strike up a liaison with them. There'll be a lot of lobbying to sit at the captain's table, or to get invited to the captain's cocktail party, or indeed any of the parties given by the ship's officers. Those who don't succeed will spend much of their time complaining to the purser about not getting invited; not getting a good seat; or about getting a cabin over the engines, or near the lifts, or by the service area.

Actually these 'holidays of a lifetime' can be a bit of a bore, hence the trend towards cruises with a theme, like bridge, music, scrabble or whatever. The advantage of being on a ship is that you don't have to come into too much contact with foreigners, although they do send you ashore from time to time to get rooked (with the purser and cruise director getting an even bigger rake-off from local souvenir shops than they take in bribes for getting you on the captain's table or even a decent table at second sitting). In practice you spend a lot more time watching the ship dock, and getting tugged out to sea again, than you do ashore.

The disadvantage of ships is that there's no way of avoiding your fellow passengers, who tend to be the hearty gin-and-tonic set, doing their best to imagine they're back in the 1930s – all cigarette holders, and dressing for dinner and parties with streamers, where the '*animateurs*' are invariably washed-out entertainers. Woe betide you if you don't join in. You're bound to get a delegation of well-meaning people knocking on your cabin door and inviting you to come and play bingo. As on smaller boats, it's life's organisers who come into their own, fixing up keep-fit sessions, flower-arranging classes, poetry readings and generally making sure everything is 'ship-shape'.

The only effective way for the Untypical Tourist to avoid all this is to spend most of the time lying on a deckchair wrapped in a blanket, looking rather pale and sick (which he probably feels) and generally giving the impression he hasn't got long to live, as he warms his hands round his mug of bouillon.

17
Going Home

'We shall not cease from exploration
And the end of all our exploring
Will be to arrive where we started
And know the place for the first time'
T. S. Eliot, *The Four Quartets*

THE BEST journey of all, of course – perhaps the only good journey – is the journey back. No pleasure experienced on your holiday will be quite as intense as the pleasure of going home. It's something a great many tourists, both Typical and Untypical, will spend most of their holiday looking forward to. Getting back to where we started is, after all, the whole point of the exercise.

This remains true, however awful the journey home turns out to be. You may, for instance, spend six hours at Ouzo Airport because the plane you're waiting for was delayed leaving Heathrow. But when at last you do clamber aboard (ranting about the foulness of Ouzo Airport rather than the foul behaviour of London's air-traffic controllers) you'll usually be ready to forgive. And when the British Airways crew give you the sort of 'Welcome Aboard' smile which says 'Aren't you glad to be flying the flag and out of the hands of all those terrible foreigners', many Typical Tourists find themselves contentedly agreeing. It doesn't take much to make a returning tourist happy – just an English newspaper offered by an English-speaking stewardess. It may not be his favourite paper, and it may be yesterday's, but it's an English paper nonetheless, with the cricket scores in; and it didn't cost him a fiver.

Even on one of those Channel crossings with twenty-foot waves, where the predominant scent and sound comes from green-faced people vomiting over the side, there'll be certain consolations. There'll be the Dave Allen cassette that they play on the telly: even if you have seen the show before, it'll be a relief after all that Ouzo folk-dancing. And even though he may be feeling a bit queasy, the Typical Tourist will probably be tempted to tuck heartily into a real 'English Breakfast'; the bacon may be mostly fat, the fried egg burnt around the edges, the sausage pink, thick-skinned and underdone, the tomato hardly worthy of the name, and it'll all be swimming in grease and very very expensive – but, the Typical Tourist will tell himself enthusiastically, it's better than that foreign muck any day. The teacup may be cracked and stained, but at least it's an improvement on those foreign glasses in chrome holders which burn your fingers when you try to pick them up; and at least the tea is made with your actual leaves, not some miserable bag that hardly manages to turn the water yellow. It's also nice to get some proper HP sauce with your meal – instead of that oregano stuff.

Perhaps the keenest pleasure of the return journey is the pleasure of anticipation – of the further culinary delights that lie in store at home, of finally learning the answer to all those questions that have been plaguing you for the previous three weeks: did you remember to cancel the milk, switch off the immersion heater, close the kitchen window, switch on the video recorder?

However, the homecoming itself can sometimes be a bit of an anticlimax, living up to all your worst expectations. You arrive back to find you *did* forget to cancel the papers; or that your houseplants *have* died; or that your neighbours did *not* look after your pets; or that the burglars *have* been; or that the squatters *have* moved in.

And there'll be other unpleasant surprises. You'll find that the weather is as awful as it always used to be. Your holiday pictures haven't come out quite as you had hoped. Your local antique dealer will tell you that the 2,000-year-old Rosetta Stone you bought from a tomb robber (or tourist robber rather) is more like two years old, if that.

And when you first set foot again on British soil, it doesn't always immediately seem like Paradise Regained. You get the same unfriendly stare from the British customs and passport officials that you did from those foreign apparatchiks. It's not 'Welcome Home', but 'Are you resident in this country?' If anything, they seem even more likely than foreign officials to suspect you of 'intent to defraud' and even less likely to believe your story that you thought it was all right to bring in the extra bottle if you'd taken a swig out of the top first. They're certainly every bit as good as foreigners at pulling everything out of your luggage so that it's impossible to repack.

You've also got to face all those people who asked you to buy something for them, or to look someone up for them, and to confess to them that you failed in your mission.

And coming home can be hard work – especially persuading people that you had the time of your life, and that everything really was wonderful. Really it was. You won't mention, of course, that you kept your watch on British time throughout the holiday, that you couldn't get the English League football scores, and that you were more than once heard to mutter the standard tourist refrain: 'I'll be glad to get home. I really will'.

But you'll have survived. And that, as we said at the outset, is what it's all about. At least you won't have to go again for a while. In fact you can congratulate yourself that you'll never have to go to Ouzo ever again, if you don't want to. Not that this will prevent you from sending your friends there. But you've been. And that of course, for the Typical Tourist (and for the Untypical Tourist as well, of course), is the great thing. Not to go. But to have been.